THREE
WOLVES

THREE
WOLVES

*A Detailed History of the American
McQuains And Their Gaelic Roots*

DAVID "TAYLOR" MCQUAIN

THREE WOLVES
A DETAILED HISTORY OF THE AMERICAN
MCQUAINS AND THEIR GAELIC ROOTS

iUniverse books may be ordered through booksellers or by contacting:

iUniverse
1663 Liberty Drive
Bloomington, IN 47403
www.iuniverse.com
844-349-9409

Because of the dynamic nature of the Internet, any web addresses or links contained in this book may have changed since publication and may no longer be valid. The views expressed in this work are solely those of the author and do not necessarily reflect the views of the publisher, and the publisher hereby disclaims any responsibility for them.

Any people depicted in stock imagery provided by Getty Images are models, and such images are being used for illustrative purposes only. Certain stock imagery © Getty Images.

ISBN: 978-1-6632-0646-6 (sc)
ISBN: 978-1-6632-0647-3 (e)

Print information available on the last page.

iUniverse rev. date: 02/18/2021

For Miriam McQuain Looker...
Whose hard work made this possible.

CONTENTS

PREFACE

The purpose of this book is to provide the future generations of Byron, Will, and Taylor McQuain with information about the origins of their surname. Thus, the title is symbolic of the three of them. The title, *Three Wolves*, is also symbolic of the countries of Ireland, Scotland, and the United States of America. These are the three countries that McQuains can trace their roots in the aforementioned order. The three wolf head crest is also a recognized symbol of Clan MacQueen of Scotland which this book will cover extensively.

Past generations have worked hard to maintain the truths found in this book through various publications and record keeping. The most noteworthy of these publications are *Tell Me a Story, Grampa, To the Front and Back a West Virginia Marine Fights World War 1, My Second War,* and *Blood of my Blood*. This book will attempt to consolidate some of the information found in these publications and others into one source to be kept and passed down to those who share the name.

I feel compelled to pass this information on to future generations due to the wealth of information that has become available to my brothers and me. The internet has had rapid growth in our lifetime and has linked us to many sources that were not previously available to our ancestors. Not passing this information down at this time would risk a complete loss in knowledge of our heritage.

This work will contain a multitude of sources, direct citations, family pictures, maps, and historical context for the periods that each McQuain lived through. Myths, rumors, and various hypotheses will also be contained in this book to inspire future generations to pursue new findings.

Unfortunately, our memories disappear with us when we go. I want to remind future generations that they too have a duty of picking up the pen and preserving the memory of our ancestors. There is a famous quote that claims, "The shortest pen is better than the longest memory." It is my hope that this short work of the pen can serve as something far more substantial than a distant memory...

TIMELINE

Life of Christ (~4BC - 36AD)
Life of Conn of the Hundred Battles (~116-136AD)
Height of the historical kingdom of Dál Riata (late 500 AD - early 600 AD)
Norse occupation of the Western Isles of Scotland (~700AD – 1264 AD)
The custom of fixed surnames commences in France (~1000AD)
Fixed surnames were introduced into Scotland through the Normans (~1100AD)
Life of Somerled (~1113-1164 AD)
MacQueens come from Ireland to Scotland as dowry for a MacDonald wedding (1314-1330)
Mora MacDonald is escorted by Raven MacQueen to marry into Mackintosh (Early 1400s)
Revan MacQueen fought with Mackintosh in Battle of Harlaw (1411)
MacQueens possess lands in Corrybrough (1500s)
MacCleods expelled from Trotternish Peninsula of Skye (1528)
MacCleods return to Trotternish Peninsula of Skye (1530s)
MacQueens assist MacDonalds with seizing Trotternish from MacCleods (May 1539)
Clan Chattan Bond- MacQueens rise in dignity to a minor clan (1609)
The sea creature ritual was performed by MacQueens in the Kilmartin, Isle of Skye. (1633)
Act for Setting Schools (1696)
The story of "The Last Wolf in Scotland" occurs (1743)
A recorded baptism of an Alexander McQuain in Inverness (2 September, 1753)
Last recorded instance of the milk ritual is practiced in the Isle of Skye (1758)
Skye's formal dance, "America", is practiced in written history (October, 1773)
Alexander sails to America (1775)

AMERICAN MCQUAINS-
PATERNAL FAMILY
TREE (REDUCED)

o Alexander McQuain (~1756-1825)

  • Alexander II McQuain (1787-1860)

    o Hugh McQuain (1817-1892)

      ▪ Thomas Charles McQuain (1852-1940)

        • Thomas Bryan McQuain (1897-1988)

          o David Brian McQuain (1935- living)

            ▪ Mark Thomas McQuain (1960- living)

              • Byron Thomas McQuain (1987- living)
              • William Dean McQuain (1988- living)
              • David "Taylor" McQuain (1990- living)

CHAPTER 1
ORIGINS

Since the title of this book denotes a history of the American McQuains, the majority of the chapters in this book will focus on known truths of the McQuain line as they dwelled in America from the 18th century onward. However, this chapter, *Origins*, will be the most sizable and will discuss the potential origins of the McQuain line based on a multitude of sources concerning Irish and Scottish history.

A common misconception in genealogical research is that "Mc" is always Irish and "Mac" is always Scottish. This is not always the case. Unfortunately, discovering truths about the McQuain name and its origins is challenging considering that no McQuain figures in the past history of Scotland or Ireland are particularly noteworthy. However, it is known that the McQuain name came to America from Scotland. American McQuains can trace their name back to one American Revolutionary War veteran and Scottish Progenitor- Alexander McQuain.

Prior to this publication, it was unclear of our exact origins other than the fact that Alexander McQuain sailed from Scotland and was born in Scotland to a Scottish family. After much research, more details have been discovered about the McQuain name. McQuains seem to have come to Scotland from Ireland. While in Ireland and Scotland, McQuains are recorded as living in areas of Norse influence. Thus, when asked by new acquaintances, "McQuain...What is that?" The proper response is: "Norse-Gaelic." By saying this, all three categories are covered.

Conducting genealogical research on small families is difficult. To make matters more difficult for McQuain genealogists, "Q" is not even a letter that is contained in the older Gaelic alphabet! In more ancient times,

Irish and Scottish Gaelic had a reduced alphabet (18 letters) and Q was not a letter that appeared in the alphabet. Thus, the Q was only added to the spelling of the McQuain surname due to English influence. This adjustment from Gaelic spelling to English spelling will be referred to frequently in this book as whenever the surname became "anglicized". It is ironic, then, that American McQuains put such emphasis on capitalizing the "Q" in McQuain.

Another difficulty that McQuain genealogists experience are the wild deviations in surname spellings that are prominent in Scottish historical records. This is mainly due to an overall lack of education in Scotland for an extended period. According to George F. Black's *Surnames of Scotland*:

> "During the Middle Ages the knowledge of the art of writing was confined largely to churchmen, and when they had occasion to record a surname there was no fixed rule of orthography to guide them. They therefore wrote down the names, especially such as were unfamiliar to them, in forms suggested by their sound…This unstable phonetic rendering of proper names continued even into the early nineteenth-century time." [1]

These deviations in surname spellings were due also to the language transition from Gaelic to English. In 1696, education in Scotland began to increase when Scottish Parliament passed the "Act for Setting Schools" which established a school in every parish in Scotland. According to Arthur Herman's *How the Scots Invented the Modern World*, this act slowly, but surely, set Scotland on an upward trajectory in English literacy:

> "The result was that within a generation nearly every parish in Scotland has some sort of school and a regular teacher. The education must have been fairly rudimentary in some places: the fundamentals of reading and grammar and nothing more. But it was available, and it was, at least in theory if not always in practice, free. Historians are still arguing about how many Scots really learned to

---

[1] George F. Black, *The Surnames of Scotland*, l.

read and write as a result of the School Act. In this, as in so many other things, the Highlands lagged far behind. But one thing is certain: Scotland's literacy rate would be higher than that of any other country by the end of the eighteenth century." [2]

This Act for Setting Schools aided in rooting out Gaelic speech in Scotland at an accelerated rate, especially in the Highlands. In 1709, there was added pressure from the Society in Scotland for Propagating Christian Knowledge (SSPCK) to anglicize Gaelic speaking Highlanders in Scotland. Since most evidence points towards "McQuain" being a Highland surname, a rapid decrease in Gaelic speech at the turn of the eighteenth century likely influenced the spelling of "McQuain". Though arguably, Gaelic was already on the decline ever since "the Scottish royal court had adopted English (or a dialect related to Middle English called Scots) back in the eleventh century, relegating Gaelic to the cultural backwater." [3] Given this transition in language, it is important to remember that we can only speculate the original Gaelic spelling and pronunciation of the "McQuain" surname due its many wild deviations in spelling. However, many of these different spelling variations are discussed in detail in this chapter. The most frequently sited possibilities in existing works are consolidated below:

MacCuinn/ O'Cuinn- (Gaelic) Meaning son of "Conn", which points back to the high kings of Ireland. Conn literally translates to "reason, wisdom" or "head/ chieftain".

MacShuibhne- (Gaelic) Meaning son of the "well-going" or "good-going", which Clan MacQueen claims as their root.

MacShuain- (Gaelic) Patronymic based on Old Scandinavian sveinn 'boy, servant', which was also used a personal name.

Sveinn- (Norse) Believed to be the name for "boy, servant".

---

[2] Arthur Herman, *How the Scots Invented the Modern World*, p. 23.
[3] Arthur Herman, *How the Scots Invented the Modern World*, p. 27.

MhicCuithein/ Clann 'ic Cuithein- (Gaelic) A minor MacDonald sept near Storr in Skye, of whom the town, BalMhicCuithein, is named.

MacCuthan/ Clann 'ic Cuithain- (Gaelic) A minor sept of MacDonalds in Skye, distinct from MhicCuithein.

Thankfully, all of the above mentioned surnames are distantly related in some way and/or generally point to the same geographic regions in Scotland. The earliest known appearances of today's spelling of "McQuain" within Scotland are from birth and baptism records discovered within the Scottish Highlands- specifically in Inverness and the Isle of Skye.

One mention is of a baptism in Inverness in 1753. This is known because on 16 July 2003 a M.Phil. Genealogical and Historical Research Consultant, named David Dobson, was hired by Mrs. Dorothy Noden to conduct research on the origins of Alexander McQuain. His findings were vast and included many different births with spelling variations such as "McQuian" and "McQueen". The results were inconclusive as none of the findings could guarantee to be the Scottish emigrant; however, there was one finding that was the exact spelling of "McQuain". In his report entitled *The MacQueen Project*, Dobson reported that in Inverness "on 2 September 1753 Alexander, son of Donald McQuain and his wife Mary Fraser was baptized." [4] It is possible that this Alexander could be our progenitor who later sailed to America to fight in the Revolutionary War. If this is true, that means that Donald McQuain and Mary Fraser of Inverness were the parents of our Alexander McQuain. However, this is just a theory. This theory also contradicts a strong source about how Alexander McQuain was born in Edinburgh. We know of this strong claim to Edinburgh because an extensive entry in a 1928 publication entitled *West Virginia, In History, Life, Literature, and Industry* by Morris Purdy Shawkee. *

The other mention is of a "M'Quain" birth in Kilmuir, Skye. The name appears in the Register of births (with no indication of date) as mentioned in George F. Black's 1946 publication entitled *Surnames of Scotland, Their Origin Meaning and History.* [5] According to a 1923 publication called

---

[4] David Dobson. *Macqueen Project*, 16 Jul 2003.

*See the Alexander McQuain chapter for full quote.

[5] George F. Black, *Surnames of Scotland, p. 559.*

Place-names of Skye and Adjacent Islands by Alexander Robert Forbes, "M'Quain" is a variant spelling of the proper name Macquien, a "small sept of no great renown" located in Balmacquien. [6] The Gaelic spelling of this surname is MhicCuithein and the Gaelic spelling of their town is BalMhicCuithein, located in the Northeast corner of Skye.

Given these appearances of "McQuain" in both Isle of Skye and Inverness records, it seems logical to deduct that "McQuain" is a surname that has Scottish highland origins, given that both of these two areas fall north of the Highland boundary fault.

So have the McQuains always been Scottish?

---

[6] Alexander Robert Forbes, *Place-names of Skye and Adjacent Islands*, p. 57.

Ireland- "O'Cuinn/ MacCuinn"

Despite knowing that the McQuain name was Scottish at one point, several factors point towards the possibility of the McQuain name having Irish roots. Existing DNA research companies, surname genealogy businesses, and various published works seem to point back to the Irish name- O'Cuinn or MacCuinn.

In 2018, I submitted my DNA via saliva by mail to a popular DNA research company known as 23andMe. After 2 months of waiting, my results on 23andme.com indicated that I bear a branch of haplogroup R-M269 and thus share a paternal-line ancestor with Niall of the Nine Hostages, one of the high kings of Ireland. The science backing the particulars of this claim can be read extensively through reading Howard and McLaughlin's 2011 publication entitled *A dated phylogenetic tree of M222 SNP haplotypes: exploring the DNA of Irish and Scottish surnames and possible ties to Niall and the Uí Néill kindred.* [7]

Genetics aside, during a trip to Scotland with my wife in 2019, there was a family name booth that was set up on one of the top floors at Edinburgh Castle for tourists to ask questions about their surname and heritage. The employees at this name booth were using a computer to find their information with a display monitor that faced the inquiring tourists. I noticed that the name of the website/database that they were using was called "House of Names.com". When I inquired about the "McQuain" name, the castle employees informed us that the McQuain name was a deviation of the Irish family O'Cuinn.

O'Cuinn literally translates to "Son of Conn". Conn, known formally as "Conn of the Hundred Battles", was a High King of Ireland. Niall of the Nine Hostages, whose descendants were the Uí Néill Dynasty, was a direct descendant of "Conn of the Hundred Battles". This theory of McQuains tracing their origins to the O'Cuinn family seems to compliment the previous information about haplogroup R-M269 because it stands to reason that the common ancestor of all (R-M269 carrying) McQuain men could be "Conn of the Hundred Battles".

A simple google search (google is today's leading internet search engine) will provide the same "O'Cuinn" result when you type "McQuain" in the

---

[7] http://regarde-bien.com/Familia.pdf

search bar. One of the top results of the google search is "House of Names. com" (the same site that the castle employees utilized) which offers the same Irish claim:

> The Irish name McQuain was originally written in a Gaelic form as O Cuinn, which means descendant of Conn... The surname McQuain was first found in county Longford (Irish: An Longfort) traditionally known as Annaly or Teffia, and situated in the Irish Midlands, in Northwest Leinster where they were Lords of Muintir Gillagain. The O'Quinns and MacQuinns (and all of the spelling variables derived from these) were descended from Conn, who in turn was descended from the Princes of Annaly... The Middle Ages saw a great number of spelling variations for surnames common in the Irish landscape. One reason for these variations is the fact that surnames were not rigidly fixed by this period because the general population had to rely on local official's understanding of how their name should be spelt, hence spellings in records often changed through a person's lifetime. The following variations for the name McQuain were encountered in the archives: O'Quinn, Quin, Quinn, Quine, MacQuin, MacQuinn, McQuin, McQuinn, MacCuin, Cuinn, Cuin and many more.[8]

To be fair, companies like "House of Names" and "23andme" profit from making claims of any kind. Therefore, this Irish theory could be an example of historical corruption that has occurred to the McQuain name due to corporate greed. However, the relationship between the surname feedback and the genetic feedback seem to complement one another and offer a plausible hypothesis that the McQuains have ancient Irish origins dating back to 2nd century AD.

Fortunately there are existing publications that further compliment the Irish theory. In *Place-names of Skye and Adjacent Islands*, Forbes definitively

---

[8] https://www.houseofnames.com/McQuain-family-crest

claims that M'Quains are MacCuinns.[9]* Forbes making this claim would indicate that, if true, McQuains originated from Ireland and can trace lineage to Conn and the Irish high kings.

Conn of the Hundred Battle's is known for his many battles and eventually possessing northern Ireland as whole:

> As Conn's title suggests, his reign was filled with battling. Conn's strenuous militancy and the suggestive title that won for him, made him famed beyond worthier men- famed through the generations and the centuries-so that it was the greatest pride of some of the noblest families of the land a thousand years and more after his time to trace their descent to him of the Hundred battles[10]...Conn, with his allies, the Degades, was defeated in ten battles- till at length, for peace sake, he had to grant to Mogh one-half of Ireland- the southern half, henceforth to be known as Leth Mogha, Mogh's half- dominion over which was claimed by Mogh's successors, through almost ten centuries following. The northern half, which he retained under his own rule is since known as Leth Cuinn, Conn's Half.[11]

The first "son of Conn" or "MacCuinn" was Conn's son, Art Mac Cuinn, also known as Art the Lonely, and one of the high kings of Ireland. Art "was known as Art the Lonely, because, as the story goes, that from the time he lost his brothers, Connla and Crionna- both slain by their uncles (though another famous story has it that Connla sailed away to Fairyland and never returned), he was pitifully solitary, and silent ever after till life's end".[12]

So if McQuains have Irish origins, how did McQuains come to Scotland?

---

[9] Alexander Robert Forbes, *Place-names of Skye and Adjacent Islands*, p. 57.
*Forbes also claims that M'Quains are MacShuibne and not McQueens. However, MacShuibne is now widely accepted as the Gaelic root for the surname MacQueen. So this is an odd and self-defeating claim. The quote rather makes one believe that MacQueen and MacCuinns are related. George Black seems to clean this thought process up in *Surnames of Scotland* by claiming there are two different groups of MacQueens- one having no relation with MacCuinn and the other being from Skye, of which, M'Quain is a variant spelling.
[10] Seumas MacManus, *The Story of the Irish Race*, p. 41.
[11] Ibid, p. 42.
[12] Ibid, p. 45.

Isle of Skye - "MacQueen"

Scotland, as a whole, owes much of its culture to Ireland. The name, Scotland, is derived from the colloquial Roman term *Scoti* (or "bandits") who were actually wanderers from Ireland who called themselves "Gaels". [13] "Celtic by language and culture, the Gaels congregated in extended family groupings- the ancestors of the clans." In fact, the term "Clan" comes from the Gaelic word *Clann,* meaning "children." [14] Thus, the theory of McQuains coming to Scotland from Ireland is sound due to the fact that most Scots have Irish origins.

Many American McQuain families grew up hearing the claim that the McQuain family is heavily associated with the Isle of Skye and the surname MacQueen. This commonality between McQuains was an exciting discovery that was made when American McQuains started to become more connected through the growth of social media platforms like Facebook (the leading social media company of today). Understandably, Facebook is hardly a valid source. However, this commonality was certainly motivational and assisted with the momentum of my search.

Luckily, there are existing publications that speak of MacQueens being of the race of Conn and journeying from Ireland to Isle of Skye. According to Alexander McQueen Quattlebaum's book, <u>Clergymen and Chiefs</u>, it is likely that the MacQueens of Scotland came from Ireland sometime between 1314 and 1330 as part of the dowry of Margaret O'Cathan who married Angus Og, a MacDonald, and Lord of Kintyre. Margaret O'Cathan was the daughter of Conn Buidhe O'Cathan who was one of the great barons of Ulster, lord of Mivady, and master of the County of Derry. Once in Scotland, the MacQueens are documented as being associated with the MacDonalds. According to Frank Adam's *Clans, Septs, and Regiments of the Scottish Highlands,* both the MacQueen and MacDonald families are documented as being "of the same stock" and "being of the race of Conn, or Cuinn, 'of the hundred battles.'"[15] This quote, in particular, seems to solidify the previous section's claims on Irish origins. Alexander McQueen

---

[13] Arthur Herman, *How the Scots Invented the Modern World*, p. 108.

[14] Arthur Herman, *How the Scots Invented the Modern World*, p. 122.

[15] Frank Adam, *Clans, Septs, and Regiments of the Scottish Highlands*, p. 272.

Quattlebaum's detailed summary of the MacQueens journey from Ireland to Isle of Skye is seen below:

> The MacQueens are said to have come to Scotland from Ireland as part of the dowry of Margaret O'Cathan (Tochradh nighean a'Chathanaich) that was given to Angus Og. As part of the dowry it was custom for the bride to be accompanied by some of the retainers of the father's territories. Conn Buidhe O'Cathan sent his daughter one retainer from each of 140 families from his extensive territories. There still exist other families in the Isles and on the mainland of the west of Scotland, as well as the MacQueens, who trace their origins to this source. If the MacQueens came to Scotland as part of Lady Margaret O'Cathan's dowry, it probably would have been between 1314 and 1330. There is every indication that one of the MacQueens' earliest settlements was in the district of Moidart, which is located just north of the peninsula of Kintyre. At this time Moidart was under the control of the MacDonalds. From Moidart the MacQueen family divided into two distinct branches as some of them moved to the north and others to Skye, to the west of Scotland. Since the time of Hugh, the first chief of the MacDonalds of Sleat and the third son of Alexander, the third Lord of the Isles, the MacQueens have associated with the MacDonalds and with the Isle of Skye. [16]

This section will focus solely on the MacQueens of Skye. The other "distinct branch" of MacQueens that the above passage refers to will be mentioned in the next section. They are known as the MacQueens of Corrybrough, to whom the Clan MacQueen associates. It is impossible to prove, definitively, if the American McQuains are descendants of the Skye MacQueens or the MacQueens of Corrybrough since "McQuain" birth records are found within Skye and Inverness (Corrybrough is in the immediate vicinity of Inverness). However, the MacQueens of

---

[16] Alexander McQueen Quattlebaum, *Clergyman and Chiefs*, p. 4.

Corrybrough/ Clan MacQueen claim to have roots from the Isle of Skye and Western Isles. So, regardless of the American McQuain's precise origins, it is important to first examine the Skye MacQueens in order to follow the proper chronology of the family.

My wife and I visited the Isle of Skye in 2019. Upon arrival, a bookstore owner in the city of Portree told us about a small town called "Balmacqueen" (Baile/Bal means township). The bookstore owner's last name was MacDonald and was very excited to share this information given that the MacDonalds and MacQueens of Skye have such a strong and historic relationship. After the conversation ended, my wife and I traveled to Balmacqueen equipped with a map we purchased from him. Upon arrival, we noticed the sign on the street was labeled- "Baile MhicCuithein" in Gaelic and "Balmacquien" in English. This was odd given the store owner and map had labeled this town as "Balmacqueen" and not "Balmacquien". When "MhicCuithein" is properly pronounced in Gaelic it sounds remarkably close to how McQuain is pronounced today! In Gaelic, the letter "C" makes a *k* sound and "Th" when flanked with vowels denotes a strong breathing sound. [17] In fact, "in Gaelic names, *th* is often a mere phonetic device for dividing syllables." [18]

"Macquien", mentioned above, has an entire section dedicated to it within Forbes' *Place-names of Skye* in the same section where the surname M'Quain is mentioned as a variant spelling. [19] Both Forbes and Black raise issue with Macquien being "erroneously rendered MACQUEEN." [20] Ironically, however, Black, himself, refers to this town as "Macqueen's township" in *Surnames of Scotland* in a section on the MacCuitheins and sites Forbes when he does it! [21] This is a perfect example of the painstaking contradictions that permeate Scottish genealogy. The surname and town, in my own opinion, is my most significant genealogical finding for the American McQuains. It is a strong support for the theory that the American McQuains are directly tied to the Isle of Skye when coupled

---

[17] Robert Bain, *Clans & Tartans of Scotland*, p. 308.

[18] George F. Black, *Surnames of Scotland*, p. lviii.

[19] Alexander Robert Forbes, *Place-names of Skye and Adjacent Islands*, p. 57.

[20] George F. Black, *Surnames of Scotland*, p. 560.

[21] George F. Black, *Surnames of Scotland*, p. 483.

with Forbes' claims about the M'Quain surname being a variant spelling of Macquien.

A similar "e" variation of our surname also appears in Hugh Bodkin's last will and testament. Hugh Bodkin fought alongside with Alexander McQuain during the American Revolutionary War. Eventually, Hugh Bodkin gave his daughter in marriage to Alexander McQuain following the war. In Hugh Bodkin's will, Alexander McQuain's surname is spelt "McQuein". It is likely that Hugh Bodkin, a graduate of the University of Dublin[22], knew the proper anglicized spelling of McQuain, so it seems logical this "e" variation of the surname in his last will and testament can be trusted. Unfortunately, even the spelling variation appearing in Hugh Bodkin's will is different from the sign located in Isle of Skye because the "i" and the "e" are reversed!

According to the bookstore owner in Portree, the MacQueens of Skye did not have the best reputation. He claimed that MacQueens of Skye were known for black magic/ witchcraft. Several books that my wife and I bought from his store support this claim.* Most all of these books use "MacQueen" and "MhicCuithein" interchangeably, further demonstrating that the MacQueens of Skye are indeed the same as the MhicCuitheins/Macquiens/M'Quains. Most all of these books also point to the MacQueens having close ties with the MacDonalds.

The pagan rituals that the MacQueens were accused of performing are likely due to the customs and religious superstition passed down to them from Viking influence during the Norse occupation of the Western Isles of Scotland. After all, the Vikings arrived in Scotland in the 8th century and reached the Hebrides shortly after.[23] In fact, sources claim that even when the Norse were expelled from most of Scotland in 10th century, "they still held their ascendancy over the Western Isles" and "with periods of varying success the Norse occupation continued until about 1264." [24]

Some sources even indicate "the Skye surname Macqueen is of Norse origin from the personal name *Sveinn*" and "lived in the Outer Hebrides

---

[22] Morris Purdy Shawkee, *West Virginia, In History, Life, Literature, and Industry*, p. 239.
* These books are quoted in detail in the chapter entitled *MacQueen Legends*.
[23] Karen Hardy and Martin Wildgoose, *Traveling Through Time*, p. 12.
[24] Robert Bain, *Clans & Tartans of Scotland*, p. 12-13.

before they lived in Skye." [25] [26] Norse and Gaelic families blended together for centuries in Ireland and much of the Scottish Highlands due to countless intermarriages between Norse and Gaelic peoples. In fact, most all families that hail from the Inner and Outer Hebrides are Norse-Gaelic due to the prolonged period that the Vikings held the Western Isles of Scotland.

Inter-clan disputes on the Isle of Skye were frequent. The most notable rivalry on the Isle of Skye was between two major clans: the MacLeods and the MacDonalds. [27] As mentioned previously, the MacQueens had strong ties to the MacDonalds in Skye. The hatred between the MacDonalds and the MacCleods was so strong that in the late 1300s, John, the 3rd Chief of Clan MacLeod "order his daughters to be buried alive in the dungeon of his castle" in order to nullify a planned wedding between two MacQueen men and his two daughters. After he buried his daughters he seized the two young MacQueens and "flogged them so savagely 'that there was scarcely a spark of life left in them,' when they were hurled from the precipice to be drowned in a stormy sea." [28]

The history behind Balmacqueen/Balmacquien needs more research but is likely due to the MacQueens assistance to the MacDonalds in taking back the Trotternish Peninsula of Skye (which contains Balmacqueen in its northern most tip) from the MacCleods in the 16th century.

Another possible explanation for Balmacqueen is found in Surnames of Scotland claiming that, "Ruaraidh Duabh Maccuithean was a story-teller to Lord MacDonald, from whom he had free lands for his service." [29] Further details on the MacQueens retaining Balmacqueen is mentioned in Frank Adam's *Clans, Septs, and Regiments of Scottish Highlands* as being under "the condition of giving a certain number of salmon yearly at a fixed price to the proprietor." [30]

---

[25] Alexander McQueen Quattlebaum, *Clergymen and Chiefs*, p. 4.

[26] George F. Black, *Surnames of Scotland*, p. 559.

[27] Karen Hardy and Martin Wildgoose, *Traveling Through Time*, p. 13.

[28] Alexander McQueen Quattlebaum, *Clergymen and Chiefs*, p. 4.

[29] George F. Black, *Surnames of Scotland*, p. 483.

[30] Frank Adam, *Clans, Septs, and Regiments of the Scottish Highlands*, p. 271.

But don't sources indicate that Alexander McQuain came to America from Edinburgh? Wouldn't that mean we are more likely related to the MacQueens of Corrybrough? Or did the MacQueens of Skye move southeast?

Corrybrough - Clan MacQueen

As mentioned in Quattlebaum's work in the previous section, there was another group of MacQueens that eventually settled in Corrybrough. Corrybrough is a region of Scotland that is slightly south of Inverness. This group of MacQueens were described in Alexander McQueen Quattlebaum's work as being a distinct and separate branch from the MacQueens that remained on the Isle of Skye. However, the MacQueens of Corrybrough, as they are called, are recorded as having roots in the Isle of Skye. In the early 1400s, some MacQueens are recorded moving East due to the marriage of Mora MacDonald and Malcom MacKintosh. A group of MacQueens, led by Revan MacQueen, were thought to have been provided as an escort for Mora MacDonald during her travels. Once Mora MacDonald was delivered and married, these MacQueens settled in Findhorn and would later occupy a great deal of land in Corrybrough. Since Revan MacQueen's arrival in Corrybrough, these MacQueens formed as a small clan known as Clan MacQueen (sometimes referred to as Clan Revan) and pledged loyalty to the Mackintosh Clan and eventually Clan Chattan. According to Robert Bain's *Clans & Tartans of Scotland*:

> The CLAN MACQUEEN were of West Hebridean origin and originally appear to have been associated with Clan Donald. The name is found in many forms, Cuinn, Suibne, Sweyn, MacCunn, MacSween, MacSuain, and MacSwan. In the 13th century there were MacSweens in Argyllshire at castle Sween, and the name remained in that district in form of Sween and Macqueen for three or four hundred years thereafter. Macqueens, Macswans, and MacSweens are numerous in Skye and Lewis, and the Macqueens held the lands of Garafad in Skye for several centuries. Early in the 15th century when Malcolm, tenth chief of the Mackintoshs, married Mora MacDonald of Moidart, the bride was accompanied by several of her clansmen, including Revan MacQueen, who settled in Mackintosh country and subsequently formed septs of the Clan Chattan. Revan Macqueen fought under Mackintosh at the Battle of

Harlaw 1411. The Macqueens settled in Strathdearn, and in the 16th century we find them in possession of the lands of Corrybrough, and figuring prominently in the district. The Clan Chattan Bond of 1609 was signed by Donald Macqueen of Corrybrough, for himself, and taking full burden of John Macqueen in Little Corrybrough and Sween Macqueen in Raigbeg. The lands of Corrybrough passed out of the possession of the Macqueens in the 18th century.[31]

It is my own logical assumption that the existence of the 3 wolf-head crest for the MacQueen family (seen at the end of this chapter) originates from these three distinct names of Donald, John, and Sween who are all mentioned in the Clan Chattan Bond of 1609. In fact, the MacQueen family's association with dogs/canines can also be attributed to their long lasting occupancy and defense of the Trotternish peninsula of Skye against various on comers- as the men who defended the peninsula were often called the "Dogs of Totternish". The wolf-head, itself, is something that started to become associated with Clan MacQueen due to a well-documented story that occurred over 100 years following the Clan Chattan Bond. This story takes place in 1743 during a meeting held by the Lord of Clan MacKintosh with regard to a wolf who was reported to be killing children in the province of Morayshire at the time. MacQueen of Pall à Chrocain, a legendary Highland deerstalker, was late to the meeting. When he arrived late, he was greeted with anger by all who were at the meeting only to reveal from under his garment the head of the wolf. This story is often referred to as the killing of the last wolf in Scotland. Of note, the Inverness baptism of Alexander McQuain mentioned in the beginning of this chapter in *The MacQueen Project* took place 10 years following this story of the wolf. The story of the last wolf of Scotland is mentioned in detail below:

One winter's day, about the year before mentioned, Macqueen received a message from the Laird of Macintosh that a large "black beast," supposed to be a wolf, had appeared in the glens, and the day before killed two children, who, with their mother, were crossing the hills

[31] Robert Bain, *Clans & Tartans of Scotland*, p. 228

from Calder; in consequence of which a "tainchel," or gatherin to drive the country, was called to meet at a tryst above Fi-Giuthas, where Macqueen was invited to attend with his dogs. Pall-a-chroacain informed himself of the place where the children had been killed, the last tracks of the wolf, and the conjectures of his haunts, and promised his assistance. In the morning the "Tainchel" had long assembled, and Macintosh waited with impatience, but Macqueen did not arrive; his dogs and himself were, however, auxiliaries too important to be left behind, and they continued to wait until the best of a hunter's morning was gone, when at last he appeared, and Macintosh received him with irritable expression of disappointment.

"ciod e a chabhag?"-"what was the hurry?" said Pall-a-chrocain.

Macintosh gave an indignant retort, and all present made some impatient reply. Macqueen lifted his plaid, and drew the black bloody head of the wolf from under his arm-

"Sin e dhuibh"-"there it is for you!" said he, and tossed it on the grass in the midst of the surprised circle.

Macintosh expressed great joy and admiration, and gave him the land called Sean-achan for meat to his dogs.[32]

The Macintosh family was not the only Highland family that favored the MacQueens. The Frasers also held the MacQueens in high regard. A certain "little Simon McQuian" (with the "i" and "a" reversed) is mentioned in several archived letters recorded by the Transactions of the Gaelic Society of Inverness. In these letters, Simon McQuian is mentioned as being a "fit" foot-man (house servant) for the young Simon Fraser who was the son of the

---

[32] Robert Chambers, *Domestic Annals of Scotland: From the Revolution to the Rebellion of 1745*, p. 609.

famous Lord Lovat of Clan Fraser.[33] This same Simon McQuian character is also mentioned in Mary Fraser's novel *The Last Highlander*. Interesting enough, the Table of Contents of *The Last Highlander* has the spelling "McQuain" listed for this character. Other sources make mention of how the other leadership within Clan Fraser favored the MacQueens, as a whole, "Donald Fraser's grandson, also Donald, during a long life was closely attached to the Macqueens, for whom he had that admiration, fidelity, and respect, so characteristic of the old Highlanders. It was affectively said of him: - 'If you want to put a smile on Donald Fraser's face, talk about Captain Macqueen and family.'" [34] The Frasers, being renowned in the highlands to this day, further prove that the MacQueens have a long history of winning favor with Highland Clans to whom they owed their allegiance. However, it is the MacDonalds that perhaps possess the greatest and longest ties of allegiance with the MacQueens above all other clans. This bond is expressed in the following quote made by Lord MacDonald of Sleate during a commissioning ceremony of a Donald MacQueen within a Highland Regiment: "It does me great honour to have the sons of chieftains in the regiment, and as the Macqueens have been invariably attached to our family, to whom we owe our existence, I am proud of the nomination."[35]

In the early 1700s, MacQueens and McQuins fought against the English and were even sold to the states as indentured servants due to their participation in highlander battles against the English crown in the Battle of Preston and in the Battle of Culloden. However, the Highlander way of life and the clan system was largely disrupted "on the afternoon of 16th April, 1746, when the attenuated battalions of half-starved clansmen composing the army of Prince Charles Edward sustained their first defeat at the hands of the troops of Duke of Cumberland on the disastrous field Culloden." [36] This defeat altered the future of Scotland and forever ended the autonomous existence of the Scottish Highland Clans. After Culloden, an Act of Parliament in 1746 even outlawed the wearing of the highland dress. This law wasn't repealed until 1782.

---

[33] Transactions of the Gaelic Society of Inverness, Volume 13, p. 139-147.

[34] Charles Fraser Mackintosh, *Confederation of Clan Chattan its Kith and Kin*, p. 81.

[35] Frank Adam, *Clans, Septs, and Regiments of the Scottish Highlands*, p. 272.

[36] Robert Bain, *Clans & Tartans of Scotland*, p. 24.

The American McQuains should care very little about the wearing of a particular Clan tartan or Clan kilt given our spelling variation from Clan MacQueen. But the main reason that American McQuains should care very little about our tartan is because "a common *clan* tartan is a modern custom dating no earlier than the late eighteenth century." [37] Thus, the family tartan tradition began in the period of time after Alexander McQuain had already left Scotland. In fact, there is "no present clear evidence that these clans, or named tartans existed before the middle of the eighteenth century." [38] Certain authors support this claim by stating, "Genuine Highlanders wore plaids in any color that pleased them, regardless of their clan."[39] In conclusion, the clan tartan phenomenon was something that did not gain popularity until the McQuains had already grown roots in America. However, if the opportunity presents itself and a tartan must worn, given this chapter's information, the MacQueen tartan would be a suitable fit and choice. The MacQueen chief and family line for the position of chief is "resident in New Zealand, and no effort has been made to establish the claim." [40]

Clan MacQueen's crest, moto, plant badge, and tartan are seen below:

41

Motto- Constant and Faithful. [42]

Crest Badge- "A wolf rampant ermine holding a pheon gules point downward argent." [43]

Heraldic Terms-

---

[37] Robert Bain, *Clans & Tartans of Scotland*, p. 26.
[38] J. Telfer Dunbar, *The Costume of Scotland*, p. 105.
[39] Arthur Herman, *How the Scots Invented the Modern World*, p. 129.
[40] Frank Adam, *Clans, Septs, and Regiments of the Scottish Highlands*, p. 272.
[41] Charles Fraser Mackintosh, *Confederation of Clan Chattan its Kith and Kin*, p. 63.
[42] Robert Bain, *Clans & Tartans of Scotland*, p. 228.
[43] Ibid

"Rampant"- said of beast standing upright on hind legs; rearing.
"Ermine"- white with black triangular spots.
"Pheon"- broad barbed arrow.
"Gules"- red. "Argent"- silver. [44]

Plant Badge- Boxwood, Red Whortleberry. [45]

MACQUEEN.

46

[44] Robert Bain, *Clans & Tartans of Scotland*, p. 317.
[45] Robert Bain, *Clans & Tartans of Scotland*, p. 229.
[46] Charles Fraser mackintosh, *Confederation of Clan Chattan its Kith and Kin*, p. 63.

CHAPTER 2

ALEXANDER MCQUAIN

(~1756-1825)

American McQuains are fortunate to know their Scottish Progenitor's name and various dates associated with certain moments in his life. This chapter will focus on all known sources that mention Alexander McQuain, the Scot who traveled to America and from whom all American McQuains can trace their lineage. While some of his earlier life remains a mystery, certain publications paint a vivid picture of his life.

Perhaps the most detailed mention of Alexander McQuain out of any publication is an entry found in a 1928 publication entitled *West Virginia, In History, Life, Literature, and Industry* by Morris Purdy Shawkee:

> This Alexander McQuain was born in the historic old City of Edinburgh, Scotland, a son of parents of wealth and education who, cherishing the hope that he would choose the church as a career, educated him with this end in view, and early in 1775 he was graduated from the theological and classical department of the University of Edinburgh, and seemingly his future was assured. It was, however, a time of great unrest throughout Great Britain, and intelligent and ambitious young men like Alexander McQuain could not fail to note, with other changing events of the times, the unmistakable attitude of the American colonies in their determination to free themselves from the injustice and domination of the mother country. This

brave resolution seemed to find an echo in the young Scotch student, and quickly determining to throw in his lot with the struggling colonists he confided only in the one who had always proved helpful his mother, and with the assistance secured passage across the sea and landed in the City of Philadelphia but a few days before the Declaration of Independence was signed. He immediately joined the Colonial army and his faithful service was given at Brandywine, Monmouth, Saratoga, the surrender of Burgoyne and the final British surrender at Yorktown, a faithful supporter of General Washington during that memorable winter at Valley Forge. [47]

This extended quote contains of wealth of information and offers a great deal of material to conduct further research. There is no official birth record that has been found to support this claim of Alexander McQuain being born in Edinburgh. However, there is another publication that agrees with this claim. In *Blood of Our Blood*, a 2003 genealogical publication, there is an entire section that mentions Alexander McQuain as being "born circa 1740, Edinburg, Scotland" and dying on "17-Apr-1826, buried 20-Apr-1826, Near Moyers, West Virginia." [48] However, c. 1756- c.1825 are inscribed on the Alexander McQuain monument located in the McQuain-Wees Cemetery.

The extended quote above states that Alexander was from a family of wealth and education. However, wealth and education were not as synonymous as one might think in 18th century Scotland. According to Arthur Herman, "between 1720 and 1840 the college student population of Scotland *trebled*. Knowledge of Latin was usually enough to get you in, and many students learned this at their parish schools. A university education was also relatively cheap." [49] So just because Alexander is known to have been college educated, does not mean he was wealthy. More research

[47] Morris Purdy Shawkee, *West Virginia, In History, Life, Literature, and Industry*, p.239.
[48] Francis McQuain Lessley Clemmer, *Blood of Our Blood*, p. 177.
[49] Arthur Herman, *How the Scots Invented the Modern World*, p. 25.

is needed on Alexander's father and mother. Currently, no publication can be found that lists the full names of Alexander's parents.

If the McQuains were from old money in Scotland, it would be particularly exciting to research if past generations of McQuains participated or helped fund the failed Darien Scheme to colonize Caledonia in Panama. "This Darien venture cost more than two thousand lives and over 200,000 pounds. It also broke the bank, literally. The loss of so much hard currency, and the ruin of so many families and business concerns that had been tied up with the Darien scheme, pushed the still-struggling Bank of Scotland over the edge. In December 1704 it suspended payments to creditors. With the kingdom's finances in tatters, and its agriculture in the grip of famine and starvation, Scotland's ruin was complete." [50] This was arguably the culminating event that led to the Union of Parliaments in 1707. Scotland had no choice but to unify with England after such an economic disaster. If the Darien Scheme succeeded, Scotland could have possibly remained a sovereign nation.

Assuming the McQuains were not from old money, it is possible that a college education, itself, could have been the vehicle that lifted the McQuain family out of Highland poverty. Perhaps the Skye McQuains, particularly ones who practiced paganism, were sent to University of Edinburgh School of Divinity in the early 1700s by some sort of popular demand or hierarchical ruling. This theory is plausible given that the passing of the Act for Setting Schools took place in 1696 and the formation of SSPCK occurred in 1709. Such vehicles would have swiftly exposed paganism and could have offered drastic solutions for such deplorable behavior.

Perhaps, the McQuain's wealth was somehow attributed to the Clan system. Perhaps, after the collapse of the Highland way of life following the defeat at Culloden, the Inverness McQuains (being a previous sept, and thus tasksmen, of either Clan Chattan, Clan Mackintosh, or Clan MacQueen) re-inherited their role of tasksmen for new private land owners. Tacksman, being the middle men between lairds and crofters, had the responsibility of maintaining crofters (workers) to meet the high rent of the laird. However, unreasonably high rent of lands was one of the leading causes of emigration from Scotland to the colonies in the 1700s. Thus,

---

[50] Arthur Herman, *How the Scots Invented the Modern World*, p. 35.

tacksman had the responsibility of discouraging emigration so they could maintain workers to keep the economy afloat. This could have been the reason that Alexander is mentioned as "confiding" in his mother, instead of father, who certainly would not have endorsed the decision to emigrate if he was indeed a Clan tacksman.

Many sources compliment the fact that there were wealthy Scottish emigrants in 1770s, despite the main reason for emigration being poverty. "It is clear that the great governing cause of emigration from Highlands in the middle of fifty years of the eighteenth century was poverty- the kind of poverty that arises from a growing population pressing upon limited agricultural and industrial resources. This remains true in spite of the unusually large number of comparatively prosperous emigrants who left for America in the early 1770's." [51] Alexander McQuain certainly could have been part of this unique group of prosperous emigrants.

The extended quote from *West Virginia, In History, Life, Literature, and Industry* mentions that Alexander arrived in Philadelphia "a few days" before the Declaration of Independence was signed. A few days is an extremely vague description. However, we know that Alexander could not have traveled after the governmental prohibition of emigration in September 1775. We also know from the extended quote that Alexander graduated from University of Edinburgh in early 1775. Thus, Alexander's arrival in Philadelphia had to be in-between early 1775 and September 1775. This logical deduction is confirmed in *Blood of Our Blood*, when it states that Alexander McQuain "immigrated to Philadelphia in 1775." [52] It is also worth noting that there is no publication that claims the exact port of debarkation for Alexander's journey to Philadelphia. Thus, despite Alexander's roots in Edinburgh, he could have sailed from a different city.

Several Scottish ports facilitated emigration in the 1770s. Many stories are documented of Highlanders traveling in mass groups from the same locality to ports of debarkation. According to *Colonist's from Scotland: Emigration to North America, 1707-1783*:

> By the 1770's the Highlander had come to look upon America as a veritable paradise of cheap land, low

---

[51] Ian Charles Cargill Graham, *Colonists from Scotland*, p. 42.
[52] Francis McQuain Lessley Clemmer, *Blood of Our Blood*, p. 177.

taxes, cheap provisions, and high wages, where beggary was unknown and the climate healthy. Such a group, apparently without a tacksman to lead them, foregathered at Killin, in Perthshire, in May, 1775. Thirty families came together, making in all over three hundred people. They spent a night in barns and outhouses and early the next morning assembled to the sound of bagpipes. Dressed in their best attire and some of them armed in the Highland fashion in spite of the law, they settled the order of march, bade farwell to their friends and relatives, and set off down the road. The first day carried them twenty-five miles to Loch Lomond. They traveled down the loch in boats for a further twenty-four miles, marched a few more miles to Dumbarton, sailed across the Clyde, and took ship at Greenock for the New World. About the same time, two hundred persons rendezvoused at Aviemore in Badenoch and marched off for Greenock to embark for America. Among them was a woman of eighty-three, on foot; her son preceded her Playing "Tullochgorum" on his bagpipes. Some of the emigrants took along children a month old, who were carried in baskets on their fathers' backs. [53]

This group that traveled together could have very well included Alexander within its ranks given the time of its occurrence. Another reason that this particular group could have contained Alexander is that this group is reported as being reasonably wealthy. Many of them are reported as possessing two hundred to three hundred pounds and being "full of good cheer, carrying themselves 'not like people flying from the face of poverty; but like men who were about to carry their health, their strength, and little property, to a better market.'" [54] [55] Assuming that this

---

[53] Ian Charles Cargill Graham, *Colonists from Scotland*, p. 75.

[54] Ian Charles Cargill Graham, *Colonists from Scotland*, p. 40.

[55] William Gilpin, *Observations, Relative Chiefly to the Picturesque Beauty, Made in the Year 1776, on Several Parts of Great Britain; Particularly the High-Lands of Scotland*, 2nd Ed. (London, 1792), I, p. 169-171.

was Alexander's ship that would mean that he left Scotland from the port at Greenock. It is also known that Alexander traveled to America with a chest of belongings. A chest that is still retained by the McQuain family to this day.

There is another mention of a ship arriving in Philadelphia in 1775 that falls into the same window of time as Alexander's arrival and as the ship mentioned above. The ship that arrived in Philadelphia is known of because it is described in detail in multiple sources:

> In June, 1775, a certain Donald McLeod petitioned the New York legislature, saying that some Highlanders had recently arrived from Scotland would gladly serve under him in defense of the liberties of the colony, 'with the Proviso of having Liberty to wear their own Country Dress Commonly called the Highland Habit.' These men, it appears, had not allowed their proscribed weapons to rust during the forced pacification of the Highlands, for McLeod reported them as being 'already furnished with Guns, Swords, Pistols and Highland Dirks which…is very necessary as all the above articles are at this time Time very difficult to be had.' Less than a year later, three Scottish merchants in Philadelphia, who took the American side in the war, 'raised companies of their own countrymen of a hundred men each, who [were] equipped in the Scottish Dress, and make a very warlike appearance. [56] [57]

An arrival of Scottish immigrants in Philadelphia that were ready to fight for the causes of liberty was a stark contrast to existing stereotypes of Scots in the 1770s. At that time there was a predominant hatred towards Scots in the colonies due to a large majority of Scots being labeled as Tories (British Loyalists). Most Highlanders/Clansmen were indeed were supporters of the British crown and had been since the French and Indian War in an attempt to make a name for themselves and build loyalty to

[56] Ian Charles Cargill Graham, *Colonists from Scotland*, p. 108,179
[57] Margaret Wheeler Willard, ed., *Letters on the American Revolution 1774-1776*, (Boston, 1925), p. 314-315

the crown following the embarrassment of Culloden. This stereotype and suspicion towards Scots was amplified by individuals like Ezra Stiles with her rally cries and publications such as "Too Much Scotism" within the colonies.

The common colonist had reason to be suspicious. Most Scottish immigrants banded together in order to increase their power and influence in the colonies. "That influence, commercial, political, and intellectual, was reinforced by a number of permanent, Scots-dominated organizations- the Scottish Charitable societies, usually called St. Andrew's clubs, which existed in several of the larger cities...the St. Andrew's Society of Philadelphia is said to have been established (1749) by a wandering member of the Charleston group." [58] Given Alexander's status, the St. Andrews society in Philadelphia could have been an organization through which he and his mother communicated with in order to secure his passage and immediate lodging. However, this is just a theory. St. Andrews Societies in the United States are still in existence today.

Shortly after Alexander arrived in America, emigration from Scotland was outlawed by the British government on September 21, 1775 and would remain outlawed till the end of the war.

Alexander's military service is well documented in many sources. However, it is unclear how exactly he came to be recruited. If Alexander McQuain was college educated, it seems odd that Alexander joined the enlisted ranks as a Private in the Army. Would he not have been a commissioned officer? Perhaps the majority of his money was spent on purchasing his way to the colonies and thus did not have the sufficient funds to purchase a commission. Or perhaps the predominant stereotypes of Scottish immigrants played a factor into his low rank.

In Section 180 of McAllister's *Virginia Militia in the Revolution*, Alexander McQuain's name is listed as a Private (above the age of 18) appearing in Captain Peter Hull's Company, Second Battalion, Augusta Militia in a 1779 muster roll.

---

[58] Ian Charles Cargill Graham, *Colonists from Scotland*, p. 131.

59

60

[59] McAllister, *Virginia Militia in the Revolution*, p. 147
[60] McAllister, *Virginia Militia in the Revolution*, p. 148,149

This excerpt confirms Captain Peter Hull's role as a commander over a troop of cavalry in the Yorktown campaign and thus Alexander McQuain's participation in the Yorktown campaign. Oren Frederick Morton's *History of Highland County, Virginia* also contains Alexander McQuain's name in a 1794 Muster under Robert McCoy's Company.

61

62

[61] Oren Frederic Morten, *A History of Highland County, Virginia*, p. 187
[62] Oren Frederic Morten, *A History of Highland County, Virginia*, p. 188

Morton goes on to state that "It is highly possible that several of the Highland militia were in the Pendleton company that marched with Governor Henry Lee to put down the Whiskey Insurrection of 1794. But in this instance there was, happily, no fighting." [63] So it is possible that Alexander McQuain also participated in that march; however, more research is needed.

According to the extended quote in *West Virginia, In History, Life, Literature, and Industry* at the beginning of this chapter, the (6) battles that Alexander took place in were: Valley Forge, Burgoyne, Brandywine, Monmouth, Saratoga, and Yorktown. However, only the last four of these six are mentioned as battles he participated in in the book- *Blood of Our Blood.*[64] Participating in any one of these battles is something that should instill great pride in future generations of McQuains. However, participating in-between four and six battles almost seems too extraordinary of an achievement and further research should be done to confirm these claims!

Currently, the only battles in which Alexander's participation is 100% confirmed through historical records is Yorktown. A mess pot, a sword, and English musket were collected by Alexander at Yorktown "as keepsakes from the war" and passed them down to his descendants. [65] These 3 items are still passed down to generations of McQuains today and seen by many. There is also a chest that was passed down through the family- the same chest that Alexander McQuain sailed from Scotland to America with. This chest's exact dimensions are mentioned in detail in "Tell Me a Story, Grandpa" along with all of the work that has been done to it to keep it functional. Miriam McQuain Looker is currently in possession of this chest.

According to Arthur Herman, the "MacDonald's 76th Highland Regiment surrendered with other British forces at Yorktown, and according to one of its officers, their captors, who included several Scottish emigrant, urged them to desert." [66] This information, coupled with the fact that Alexander McQuain gained personal property from surrendering parties

[63] Oren Frederic Morten, *A History of Highland County, Virginia*, p. 189
[64] Francis McQuain Lessley Clemmer, *Blood of Our Blood*, p. 177.
[65] Francis McQuain Lessley Clemmer, *Blood of Our Blood*, p. 177.
[66] Arthur Herman, *How the Scots Invented the Modern World*, p. 255.

at Yorktown, leads one to believe that Alexander could have likely been one of these Scottish emigrants who was urging them to desert. Alexander McQuain was one of the few Scots in Peter Hull's company and also likely aware of his own families' ties with the MacDonalds in the Isle of Skye causing this theory to be even more plausible! According to Herman, not a single one the MacDonald Highlander was seduced by these offers to desert.

Alexander later married and received lands for his service in the Revolution. His wife's name was Mary Bodkin. The particulars of his land grants are spelled out in *Blood of Our Blood* as being a grant of 52 acres in Pendleton County on the Blackthorn at the mouth Plum Run, West Virginia. He also possessed land on Jackson Mountain and land "close to the ridge". [67] The particulars of his marriage are spelled out in detail in *West Virginia, In History, Life, Literature, and Industry*:

> During his army service Alexander McQuain formed many friendships with the brave colonists he was assisting, not a few of whom were of his own nationality, but the one with whom he formed the strongest ties was one Hugh Bodkin, a highly educated man, formerly a professor in the University of Dublin, who, like himself had come to the American colonies in admiration of their principles of freedom. They later entered into closer relationship as Mr. McQuain subsequently married Miss Mary Bodkin after her return from Ireland, her father having sent her back to the old country to complete her education.[68]

Alexander and Mary McQuain had many sons and daughters. Of whom, one son was also named Alexander. This son will be referred to as Alexander II for the duration of this book. Alexander II is the continuation of our particular ancestral line. According to *Blood of Our Blood* Alexander and Mary McQuain had a total of 10 Children in the following order: [69]

---

[67] Francis McQuain Lessley Clemmer, *Blood of Our Blood*, p. 177.

[68] Morris Purdy Shawkee, *West Virginia, In History, Life, Literature, and Industry*, p.239-240

[69] Francis McQuain Lessley Clemmer, *Blood of Our Blood*, p. 177-178.

David "Taylor" McQuain

Duncan McQuain
John McQuain
William McQuain
Alexander McQuain II
Hugh Alexander McQuain
Nancy Elizabeth McQuain
Thomas McQuain
Jane McQuain
Esther McQuain
Isabella McQuain

CHAPTER 3
ALEXANDER MCQUAIN (II)
(1787- 1860)

Alexander II, son of Alexander and Mary (Bodkin) McQuain, was born on 5 April 1787 in Pendleton County VA and died in Gilmer County VA (WV) on 18 February 1860. These exact dates are supported by public records and "Blood of Our Blood" (with the exception of a conflicting birth year of 1784 in "Blood of Our Blood"). [70] According to *Tell Me a Story, Grandpa*, Alexander II served in the War of 1812. [71] However, more research will need to be done to verify the particulars of this claim. "West Virginia, In History, Life, Literature, and Industry" makes a following claim about Alexander II:

> Alexander McQuain, the second, the grand-father of Doctor McQuain, son of Alexander and Mark (Bodkin) McQuain, was born in what is now Pendleton County, West Virginia, moving into Gilmer County later in life and becoming a substantial farmer. He married Miss Elizabeth Scott, daughter of Alexander Scott, a native of Ireland, who was a soldier in the Revolutionary war and took part in the battle of Point Pleasant. [72]

---

[70] Francis McQuain Lessley Clemmer, *Blood of Our Blood*, p. 177.
[71] Miriam McQuain Looker, *Tell Me a Story Grandpa*, p. 303.
[72] Morris Purdy Shawkee, *West Virginia, In History, Life, Literature, and Industry*, p. 240.

This move to Gilmer County is well documented in *Tell Me a Story, Grandpa* and is the first story that appears in the book. It is a story that has been told for many generations. This story is nicknamed *The Panther Story*. The story tells of Alexander II's family encountering a panther while "moving from Randolph County, which was then Virginia, to Little Cover Creek in 1821. The trip was about 75-100 mile and took 3 or 4 days. They used pack horses to carry their belongings over the steep narrow roads, fording the streams."[73] These "painters", as Alexander II and family pronounced them, almost killed the McQuain dogs. The dogs were able to seek shelter under the small log house they were staying in but the panthers' claw marks were visible the next morning. Alexander II's only two boys alive at the time were Hugh and George. They were so terrified that night that they jumped into bed with their parents.

Prior to this move, Alexander II is documented as being close friends with Cummins Jackson, the uncle of "Stonewall" Jackson. Their friendship dates back to when they were children because "in their boyhood, they had lived on neighboring farms." [74] Their friendship continued even after Alexander II's move to Gilmer County as they visited one another frequently. Cummins subsequently raised his two nephews, Warren and Thomas (Stonewall), following the death of their parents.

Myra Pauline McQuain, one of Alexander II's great granddaughters, tells a story in *Tell Me a Story, Grandpa* about how Alexander II helped Cummins hide a counterfeit minting machine on the McQuain farm:

> As the story goes, Cummins made a very good grade of counterfeit money and the money poured from his mint in great quantities. He was very shrewd and it was several years before federal authorities caught up with him. He would take long trips into neighboring states, Ohio, Kentucky and Tennessee, and in in fact, had learned the counterfeiting business from a group in Tennessee. One time, when things were getting hot for him, he brought his minting machine to our great-grandfather's home [Alexander II's home] there on Big Cove, and asked him to

73 Miriam McQuain Looker, *Tell Me a Story Grandpa*, p.1.
74 Miriam McQuain Looker, *Tell Me a Story Grandpa*, p. 308

hide it until it would be safe for him to resume his money making. But Cummins brought a newer type machine later, and never came after the old one. It remained in our family's care until 20 years or more after the Civil War, when my uncle and aunt took a sledge hammer and knocked it to pieces, fearing it might cause trouble. The legislature had just passed an act declaring it unlawful to have such a machine in one's possession.

The family story says that Cummins had also brought the melting pot and silver, together with a great deal of his minted money, and had hidden them among those large rocks on the hill behind our house. Those are the ones we called Jackson Rocks. We have searched for hours in vain, trying to find this treasure.

Cummins Jackson joined the gold rush to California and died a few months after he reached the Pacific Coast. [75]

Alexander II and Elizabeth McQuain had many sons and daughters. Of whom, one son's name was Hugh. Hugh McQuain is the continuation of our particular ancestral line. According to the Census of 1830 and 1840, Alexander II and Elizabeth McQuain had a total of 9 children. Their children's names are listed below in age order:

Hugh McQuain
George Hill
Thomas M. McQuain
Jane McQuain
Cassidy McQuain
Charles J. McQuain
Rebecca W. McQuain
Nancy McQuain
William McQuain

---

[75] Miriam McQuain Looker, *Tell Me a Story Grandpa*, p. 309.

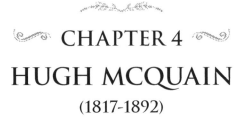

CHAPTER 4
HUGH MCQUAIN
(1817-1892)

76

Hugh McQuain was born 1817 in Gilmer County. He was a farmer, school teacher, and sheriff. Hugh McQuain married Eunice Martney

---

[76] This photo is the personal property of David "Taylor" McQuain. It was mailed to his address by Miriam McQuain Looker on April 13th, 2020 and is from a Tintype that she has "which is much darker". The back of the photograph reads "Hugh McQuain father of T.C."

36

Scott in 1848 when he was 31 years old. Eunice Martney Scott was Hugh McQuain's 1st cousin. In West Virginia, marriage to a first cousin was a common practice and socially acceptable at that time. Hugh's life, particularly in his 40s, was heavily affected by the American Civil War. According to *Tell Me a Story, Grandpa* the sympathies of the people of Gilmer and Randolph counties were divided. In those counties, there were about equal numbers serving in both armies, although West Virginia as a whole supplied far more soldiers to the North than to the South. [77] Hugh "did favor the Southern Cause, and this was known by nearly all in the county but, on the other hand, he tried to be neutral in the way he treat soldiers. Union soldiers from the area felt safe to talk to him or to visit and share a meal. At the same time, they knew that Southern soldiers of the neighborhood felt equally safe."

However, Hugh also spent a lot of time in hiding from Union soldiers. According to *Tell Me a Story, Grandpa*, when Hugh "learned the Union authorities were arresting men in the counties who were known to favor the Southern Cause, he left home and hid before they got him." [78] Hugh's children also reported stories of their mother preparing food that was never put on the table at times when they knew their father was in hiding during Union raids. [79]

Facts of Hugh's life are mentioned sporadically throughout Miriam McQuain Looker's *Tell Me a Story, Grandpa*. A specific entry about Hugh is also made in *West Virginia, In History, Life, Literature, and Industry.* The entry claims that he taught Stonewall Jackson elementary school:

> Hugh McQuain, son of Alexander and Elizabeth (Scott) McQuain, and father of Doctor McQuain, was born in Harrison County, Virginia, now Gilmer County, West Virginia, in 1817. When a young man, teaching a country school, he was much pleased with a very intelligent pupil and upright youth whose name was Thomas Jonathan Jackson, later to become the distinguished soldier, "Stonewall" Jackson, of the Confederate army in the War

---

[77] Miriam McQuain Looker, *Tell Me a Story Grandpa*, p.286

[78] Miriam McQuain Looker, *Tell Me a Story Grandpa*, p.290

[79] Miriam McQuain Looker, *Tell Me a Story Grandpa*, p.290

Between the States. Hugh McQuain became a prominent man in his county, at one time serving as county sheriff, and was an extensive farmer. His death occurred in 1892. He married Miss Eunice Scott, daughter of Thomas and Elizabeth (Skidmore) Scott, who had come to the United States from Ireland. To this marriage the following children were born: George W., Thomas C., Oliver C, Elizabeth, Alexander, Maria Columbia, Adam S., John Ewell and Mary, all born in the old homestead on the same farm. [80]

Hugh and Eunice (Scott) McQuain had many sons and daughters. Of whom, one son's name was Thomas Charles. Thomas Charles McQuain is the continuation of our particular ancestral line. In agreeance with the quote seen above and according to the Census of 1870 and 1880, Hugh and Eunice McQuain had a total of 9 children. Their children's names are listed below in age order:

George W. McQuain
Thomas Charles McQuain
Oliver C. McQuain
Nancy Elizabeth McQuain
Alexander "Zan" McQuain
Maria Columbia McQuain
Adam Scott McQuain
John Ewell McQuain
Mary D. McQuain

---

[80] Morris Purdy Shawkee, *West Virginia, In History, Life, Literature, and Industry*, p. 240.

CHAPTER 5

THOMAS CHARLES MCQUAIN

(1853- 1940)

Thomas Charles McQuain was born in 1853 in Gilmer County, WV. He spent the majority of his life as a farmer. Thomas Charles McQuain married Jessie Lewis on 26 October, 1895. Jessie Lewis was the daughter of Oliver Hazard Perry Lewis and Elizabeth (Mills) Lewis. Jessie's father, Oliver Hazard Perry Lewis, fought for the Confederate Army during Civil War and many of his stories and records have been kept by the McQuain family to include stories of when he was a prisoner of war.

Thomas Charles McQuain and Jessie (Lewis) McQuain are mentioned in great detail in *Tell me a Story, Grandpa*. The majority of the book will refer to them as 'Ma' and 'Pa' when the author, Thomas Bryan McQuain, refers to them. Ironically, while growing up on the family farm, all of Thomas Charles McQuain's children addressed him and his wife as 'Tom' and 'Jessie'. Thomas Charles McQuain's property was so spread out from neighboring farms that him and his children weren't aware that this practice was unique. The children only began calling their parents 'Ma' and 'Pa' late into their childhood based on a suggestion of a close family friend who worked on their farm. This individual's name was Sherman. Sherman assisted the McQuains with hoeing corn, putting up hay, and various other farm work. Sherman informed the children one evening that he thought the practice was bizarre and failed to show respect. That same evening, Thomas Bryan McQuain began calling his father "Pa" and did so for the first time when asking his father to spread the butter on his bread at the dinner table. [81]

Thomas Charles' appearance in *Tell Me a Story, Grandpa* is frequent as most of the stories in it take place on his farm. Thomas Charles died on 13 April 1940. Thomas Charles McQuain and Jessie (Lewis) McQuain had many children. One of these children was Thomas Bryan McQuain, of whom we are a direct descendant. According to the Census of 1920, Thomas Charles and Jessie had 8 children in the following order:

Thomas Bryan McQuain
George W. McQuain
Eunice E. McQuain
Clemmie L. McQuain
Edna C. McQuain
Helen Leah McQuain
Myra P. McQuain
Perry Hugh McQuain

---

[81] Miriam McQuain Looker, *Tell Me a Story Grandpa*, p. 5

82

CHAPTER 6

THOMAS BRYAN MCQUAIN

(1897-1988)

Thomas Bryan McQuain, the first born of Thomas Charles McQuain and Jessie (Lewis) McQuain, was born in 1897 in Gilmer County, WV. Thomas Bryan's life is well documented and arguably more immortalized than any of my ancestors. There are three books that speak extensively about his life: *Tell Me a Story, Grandpa, To the Front and Back*, and *My Second War*. His younger years leading up to 1918 on the family farm near Troy are forever captured in *Tell Me a Story, Grandpa*. Prior to the World War I, Thomas Bryan had never been 25 miles from home. Thomas Bryan volunteered for the Marines in 1918 at age 21. *To the Front and Back* is a book that speaks extensively of his experiences as an enlisted machine-gunner on the front lines on the eastern front during World War I.

During World War I, Thomas Bryan McQuain attended boot camp at Parris Island. While signing his first payroll at Parris Island, Thomas Bryan notice the name of his cousin Adam McQuain right above his own. He would later find out after the war, from his uncle 'Zan', that Adam had joined the 5th Regiment and was wounded. [83]

After Parris Island, Thomas Bryan, attended Machine Gunner School in Quantico. One of the machine gun systems that these Marines trained with extensively was Lewis light machine guns which had a drum magazine on top and were mounted on wheeled carts which could be attached to motorcycles.

"For reasons of logistics and standardization, American Expeditionary Force General John J. Pershing did not allow the Marines to take them to France. They were replaced by the hated French Chauchat light machine guns, which were not as effective." [84] The Chauchat (pronounced "Show-Sha") was a French weapon system that had a horrible reputation for its lack of accuracy. "The Chauchat, a French weapon made in a bicycle factory, was the Marines' squad and platoon automatic rifle in World War I. It weighed only 17 pounds and fired the French 8mm cartridge. Marines said it could be fired from the hip as accurately as from the shoulder- that is, 'spray and pray' for a hit." [85]

Thomas Bryan was assigned to 3rd Platoon, 80th Company, 6th Regiment, 4th Marine Brigade of the 2nd Division where his first major offensive that he participated in was the battle of St. Mihiel. In his book, Thomas Bryan recalls the terror of St. Mihiel:

> This was the biggest racket I ever heard. It sounded like thousands of blasts of dynamite in hard rock, each blast having several sticks of dynamite. They were going off everywhere, behind us, in front of us, and on all sides at the same time...The sergeant said it was the biggest barrage he had ever been in, and that was saying something since he had been in Chateau Thiery, and maybe Belleau

---

[83] Thomas Bryan McQuain, *To the Front and Back*, p. 19.
[84] H. Avery Chenoweth, *Semper Fi, The Definitive Illustrated History of the U.S. Marines*, p. 120.
[85] E. H.. Simmons and J. R. Moskin, *The Marines*, p.159.

Woods. I have learned since that this was the greatest concentration of artillery fire in the history of the world. More than 1,000,000 shells were fired in about 4 hours with a rate of 500,000 explosions per hour, 833 a minute, or 139 per second, in a front area of 20 miles in length. (Each shell has two explosions, on leaving the gun, and the other when it hits.) The troops within hearing of all this explosive power were 430,000 Americans and 70,000 French. [86]

Thomas Bryan's nickname in his unit was 'Mack'- given his last name. [87] His book is filled with stories of various objectives his unit was given, being short on supplies, trading equipment, humorous near death experiences, and horrific stories of casualties and fatalities.

Following the Battle of St. Mihiel, he advanced to the village of Limey. In Limey, Thomas Bryan was helping a fellow Marine into a trench when the Thomas Bryan lost footing and almost landed on his own bayonet. This bayonet is still in the McQuain family's possession today.

88

Also near Limey, Thomas Bryan recalls heroically volunteering to run through 300-400 yards of shelling to make contact with another unit in order to find out the name of the outfit. Thomas Bryan stated in his book that, "as I recall it, the unit was the 4th Machine Gun Battalion." [89]

Following Limey, Thomas Bryan's next objective was Jauiny-Xammes Ridge. After much fighting, around September 18th Thomas Bryan recalls coming down with a temperature of 104 degrees and going to 'sick-call'. On September 20th, he was transferred to an evacuation hospital at Remicourt.

[86] Thomas Bryan McQuain, *To the Front and Back*, p.59
[87] Thomas Bryan McQuain, *To the Front and Back*, p. 68
[88] Thomas Bryan's bayonet. Property of Taylor McQuain.
[89] Thomas Bryan McQuain, *To the Front and Back*, p. 60

This illness turned out to be the flu. His first night there in Remicourt the men on either end of his bed died in their sleep. He later made it back to his unit at noon on October 18th. When he made it back to his unit, Thomas Bryan recalls in his book that he only recognized a few Marines. "I looked over 3rd Platoon and only saw about three or four men that I knew in it. I had known nearly all in it before St. Mihiel…The outfit had been through Blanc Mont Ridge while I was away." [90]

Thomas Bryan also fought in the Argonne. Armed with a Chouchat machine gun he and 8 others were the sole survivors of his platoon of 55 before the Armistice was signed. According to his book, the eight Marines from 3rd Platoon, 80th Company, 6th Regiment, 4th Marine Brigade of the 2nd Division were: Lt. McSweeny, Pvt. Wisely, Pvt. Shell (his barrel carrier), McMillan, Cleaver, Mooney, Comax, and Sgt. Aenod. [91]

Upon return to the United States, Thomas Bryan married Opal Aldah Morrison on 30 November 1922. Thomas Bryan also went on to serve in the US Navy as a sailor in World War II, where he served in a ship repair unit. Thomas Bryan died at 11a.m. on November 11, 1988, at age 91, in Maryville Ohio. "It was fitting that he should leave us on Armistice Day, which meant so much to him." [92]

Thomas Bryan McQuain and Opal (Morrison) McQuain had a total of four children as confirmed in the Census records of 1940. One of whom is named David, of whom we are a direct descendant. All of their names are listed below in age order:

Miriam McQuain
Jesabel McQuain
Thomas McQuain
David McQuain

---

[90] Thomas Bryan McQuain, *To the Front and Back*, p. 76
[91] Thomas Bryan McQuain, *To the Front and Back*, p. 107
[92] Thomas Bryan McQuain, *To the Front and Back*, p. 262

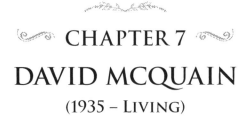

CHAPTER 7
DAVID MCQUAIN
(1935 – LIVING)

David Brian McQuain was born in 1935 in Gilmer County, West Virginia. He was the youngest of 4 children. After graduating high school in 1953, he attended Northwestern University in Illinois. In college, David majored in chemistry. After college, David McQuain married Sharon Lee Ulrey on April 13th in 1958.

David worked as a scientist for the National Cash Register Corporation (NCR) in Dayton, Ohio for 18 years. At the time, NCR was known widely known as the company that patented and introduced carbonless paper. Carbonless paper was a vital business stationary used when one or more copies had to be kept, like invoices and receipts. Prior to carbonless paper, the options were to write the document down more than once or to insert a sheet of carbon between the document being written on and the copy.

According to a phone conversation on 23 July 2020, David McQuain said that most of the projects he recalled working on while at NCR dealt heavily with photochromic compounds. While employed at NCR David developed over 1,000 new photochromic compounds. Shortly after being hired, David worked on a secret contract developing photochromic goggles for the use of pilots so that they would not go blind from a nuclear blast. David later attempted to make photochromic sunglasses. David McQuain also recalled working on a particular project that was featured in the 1964 World Fair in Queens, New York. David McQuain's project was a 1 inch by 1 inch photochromic micro-image of the entire New Testament of the Bible.

David McQuain also claims that the technology behind mood rings was also founded by NCR. In 1979, David left NCR for a small company that made mood rings. David claims that this technology is known as liquid crystal technology. David later became an entrepreneur from 1979 to 2006 by starting several companies that dealt with thermography with respect to breast cancer. David lived in Wisconsin, Illinois, and Ohio throughout the majority of his life.

David McQuain has always been known for his competitive spirit. He is constantly encouraging his children and grandchildren to play a quick game of cards with him or a board game. He was always told that he inherited this love for games from his mother's father- who was apparently an incredible card player. His energy level is always high and he is constantly smiling. However, David is truly happiest whenever he wins in a game! Most of David's grandchildren recall stories of how they would cry at a young age because David would celebrate so heavily at their failure in whatever game they were playing. This trait was always easily excusable at an older age when they could take joke. This competitive spirit always makes playing games with family even more fun! He and his wife, Sharon, have 12 grandchildren and 2 great-grandchildren. They see their family every thanksgiving during an annual Outer Banks, NC beach trip…

David McQuain and Sharon (Ulrey) McQuain had four children together. One of whom is named Mark to whom we are a direct descendant. Their children are listed below in age following order:

Mark Thomas McQuain
Kent Bryon McQuain
Barry David McQuain
Karen Ruth McQuain

CHAPTER 8

MARK MCQUAIN

(1960 – LIVING)

Mark McQuain was born in 1960 in Dayton, Ohio. After graduating high school, Mark attended Massachusetts Institute of Technology (MIT) in 1978. Mark graduated from MIT in 1982 with a degree in electrical engineering. Following MIT, Mark received his Medical Degree from Ohio State University. Mark and his wife, Dee, moved to Rochester, MN where Mark completed his residency at the Mayo Clinic. He and his wife would later move to Kansas and then to Johnson City, TN, Dee's hometown. Mark continues to work at an orthopedic practice in Johnson City, TN.

Mark Thomas McQuain is married to Dee (Owens) McQuain. They had three sons together in the following order...

Byron Thomas McQuain
William Dean McQuain
And
David "Taylor" McQuain

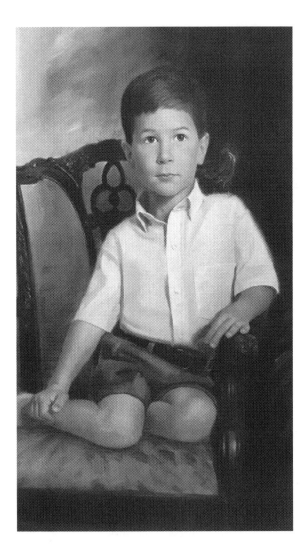

CHAPTER 9
APPENDIX

- MacQueen Legends (Isle of Skye)
- The Murder of Thomas McQuain
- Irish and Scottish Songs
- Pictures/Scanned Records

MacQueen Legends (Isle of Skye)

"The Wrestling Bout"

"Rigg was famous for a family of MacQueens, who played an important part in the past history of Skye. They were reputed of muscular proportions, and given a wide berth in quarrels. Alasdair Og, mac na Caillich, one of these MacQueens, after a strenuous struggle, overcame in a wrestling bout an Irish Champion. Before the latter could be got to a doctor, he died, and was buried at Rudha an Eireannaich (Irishman's Point) near Broadford." [93]

"Cat Roasting Ritual/ Famous Clann 'Ic Cuithein Rhyme"

"On the seashore, a mile further north from Rigg, there is a curious huge boulder. It is about 40 feet in height with a circumference of 120 feet. A wide arch penetrates through its centre. Nearby is a similar but smaller one. The former goes by the name An Eaglais Bhreige (Lying Church), and the latter a' Chubaid (Satan's Seat).

Tradition suggests pagan rites being carried out at the Eaglais Bhreige, at which his Satanic Majesty presided. Black cats were roasted alive as one of the sacrifices. A young MacQueen woman is said to have been inveigled to their rites. Her whereabouts became known to her people, who assembled and put to rout the idolatrous assemblage, rescued the young woman and removed the *cubaid*, to where it now stands. Above the Eaglis is the Grianan, a green sunny delightful stretch near the cliff's edge, with Dun Grianan about the centre, and Lon an t-Sithein skirting it till it joins the Lealt. There is a rhyme about Clann 'Ic Cuithein, who performed these pagan rites:

Clann 'Ic Cuithein[94] dhubh man briag,
Clann 'Ic Cuithein dhubh an t-sodail,

---

[93] William MacKenzie, *Old Skye Tales, Traditions, Reflections and Memories*, p.27, Birlinn Limited 2002.

[94] Other versions of this ancient saying spell the first line as the Gaelic "Clann 'Ic Cuithain"

Clann 'Ic Mhanainn dhubh na braide,
Ged nach b'fhaid' iad na cas biadaig'.
Black Clan MacCuithen[95] of the lies,
Black Clan MacCuithen of the flattery,
Black Clan Macmhannan of the theft,
Though as short as a dagger haft." [96]

"Taghairm"

"This awful ceremony to which this was given was also known among old men as 'giving his supper to the devil'. It consisted of roasting cats alive on spits till the aarch-fiend himself appeared in bodily shape. He was compelled then to grant whatever wish the persons who had the courage to perform the ceremony preferred, or, if that was the object of the magic rite, to explain and answer whatever question was put to him. Tradition in the West Highlands makes mention of three instances of its performance, and it is a sort of tribute to the fearless character of the actors that such a rite should be ascribed to them…The third instance of its performance was by some Clann 'ic Cuithein, 'the Children of Quithen', a small sept in Skye now absorbed (as so many minor septs have been) into the great family of the MacDonalds. The scene was a natural cavity called *an Eaglais Bhreige*, 'the Make-Believe Cave'[97], on the East Side, Skye. There is the appearance of an alter beside this church, and the locality accords well with the alleged rite." [98]

---

95 Other versions of this ancient saying spell the first line as the English "MacCuithan/MacCuthan"

96 William MacKenzie, *Old Skye Tales, Traditions, Reflections and Memories*, p.27-28, Birlinn Limited 2002.

97 Ronald Black corrects this in his notes at the end of the book. He says that Eaglais means 'Church' not 'Cave' on page 425.

98 Ronald Black, *The Gaelic Otherworld, John Gregorson Campbell's Superstitions of the Highlands and Islands of Scotland and Witchcraft and Second Sight in the Highlands and Islands*, p. 167, Birlinn Origin 2019.

"Sea Creature Ritual/ Famous Clann 'Ic Cuithein Rhyme"

"Martin, in his *Description of the Western Islands*, p.110, quoted by Scott (Lady of the Lake, not 2T), after describing a mode of taghairm by taking a man by the feet and arms to a boundary stream and bumping him against the bank till little creatures came from the sea to answer the question of which the solution was sought, says: 'I had an account of the most intelligent and judicious men in the Isle of Skie, that about sixty-two years ago the oracle was thus consulted only once, and that was in the parish of Kilmartin, on the east side, by a wicked and mischievous set of people, who are now extinguished, both root and branch.'

The Taghairm here referred to seems to be that the above-mentioned as having been performed by the MacQuithens in the Make-Believe or False Cave on East Side, Skye. The race have not borne a good reputation, if any value is to be attached to a rhyme concerning them and other minor septs in Skye. There is a venom and an emphasis in the original impossible to convey in a translation:

Clann 'ic Cuthain churn am briag,
Clann 'ic Cuithein chur an t-sodail,
Clann 'ic Mhannain churn a braide
Ged nach b' fhaid' iad na cas biodaig. [99]

'The MacCuthan, expert in lies, / The MacQuithens, expert in base flattery, / The MacVannins, expert as thieves / Though no bigger than a dagger handle.'" [100]

The screenshot seen below is the exact wording from "A Description of the Western Islands of Scotland" by Martin Martin (Circa 1695) concerning the above mentioned ritual:

---

[99] Notice that the spelling of Clann 'ic Cuthain in the first line differs from the previous time this rhyme was sited and also the lack of the "dhubh" (black) and the addition of "churn/chur" (sow/sowing). The English translation also differs in "dagger's handle".

[100] Ronald Black, *The Gaelic Otherworld, John Gregorson Campbell's Superstitions of the Highlands and Islands of Scotland and Witchcraft and Second Sight in the Highlands and Islands*, p. 169, Birlinn Origin 2019.

108 *A* DESCRIPTION *of the*
the Hills, given to the Forester, according to Custom.

EVERY Family had commonly two Stewards, which in their Language were call'd *Marischall Tach*: the first of these serv'd always at home, and was oblig'd to be well vers'd in the Pedegree of all the Tribes in the Isles, and in the Highlands of *Scotland*; for it was his Province to assign every Man at Table his Seat according to his Quality; and this was done without one word speaking, only by drawing a Score with a white Rod which this *Marischall* had in his hand, before the Person who was bid by him to sit down: and this was necessary to prevent Disorder and Contention; and tho the *Marischall* might sometimes be mistaken, the Master of the Family incurr'd no Censure by such an Escape: but this Custom has been laid aside of late. They had also Cup-bearers, who always fill'd and carry'd the Cap round the Company, and he himself drank off the first Draught. They had likewise Purse-masters, who kept their Mony. Both these Officers had an hereditary Right to their Office in Writing, and each of them had a Town and Land for his Service: some of those Rights I have seen fairly written on good Parchment.

BESIDES the ordinary Rent paid by the Tenant to his Master, if a Cow brought forth

Western Islands of Scotland. 109

forth two Calves at a time, which indeed is extraordinary, or an Ewe two Lambs, which is frequent, the Tenant paid to the Master one of the Calves or Lambs; and the Master on his part was oblig'd, if any of his Tenants Wives bore Twins, to take one of them, and breed him in his own Family. I have known a Gentleman, who had sixteen of these Twins in his Family at a time.

THEIR antient Leagues of Friendship were ratify'd by drinking a Drop of each other's Blood, which was commonly drawn out of the little Finger. This was religiously observ'd as a sacred Bond; and if any Person after such an Alliance happen'd to violate the same, he was from that time reputed unworthy of all honest Mans Conversation. Before Mony became current, the Chieftains in the Isles bestow'd the Cow's Head, Feet, and all the Entrails upon their Dependents; such as the Physician, Orator, Poet, Bard, Musician, &c. and the same was divided thus: the Smith had the Head, the Piper had the, &c.

IT was an antient Custom among the Islanders, to hang a He-Goat to the Boat's Mast, hoping thereby to procure a favourable Wind: but this is not practis'd at present; tho I am told it hath been done once by some of the Vulgar within these 13 Years last past.

THEY

101

110 *A* DESCRIPTION *of the*

THEY had an universal Custom, of pouring a Cow's Milk upon a little Hill, or big Stone, where the Spirit call'd *Browny* was believ'd to lodg: this Spirit always appear'd in the shape of a tall Man, having very long brown Hair. There was scarce any the least Village in which this superstitious Custom did not prevail. I enquir'd the reason of it from several well-meaning Women, who, until of late, had practis'd it; and they told me, that it had been transmitted to them by their Ancestors successfully, who believ'd it was attended with good Fortune, but the most Credulous of the Vulgar had now laid it aside. It was an ordinary thing among the Over-curious to consult an invisible Oracle, concerning the Fate of Families, and Battles, &c. This was perform'd three different ways; the first was by a Company of Men, one of whom being detach'd by Lot, was afterwards carry'd to a River, which was the Boundary between two Villages; four of the Company had hold on him, and having shut his Eyes, they took him by the Legs and Arms, and then tossing him to and again, struck his Hips with force against the Bank. One of them cry'd out, What is it you have got here? Another answers, A Log of Birch-wood. The other cries again, Let his invisible Friends appear from all quarters, and let them relieve him by giving an Answer to our present Demands: and in a few

Western Islands of Scotland. 111

few Minutes after, a number of little Creatures came from the Sea, who answer'd the Question, and disappear'd suddenly. The Man was then set at liberty, and they all return'd home, to take their Measures according to the Prediction of their false Prophets; but the poor deluded Fools were abused, for the Answer was still ambiguous. This was always practis'd in the Night, and may literally be call'd the Works of Darkness.

I HAD an account from the most intelligent and judicious Men in the Isle of *Skie*, that about sixty two Years ago, the Oracle was thus consulted only once, and that was in the Parish of *Kilmartin*, on the East side, by a wicked and mischievous Race of People, who are now extinguish'd, both Root and Branch.

THE second way of consulting the Oracle was by a Party of Men, who first retir'd to solitary Places, remote from any House, and there they singled out one of their number, and wrapt him in a big Cow's Hide, which they folded about him: his whole Body was cover'd with it except his Head, and so left in this posture all night, until his invisible Friends reliev'd him, by giving a proper Answer to the Question in hand; which he receiv'd, as he fancy'd, from several Persons that he found about him all that time. His Consorts return'd to

102

---

[101] Martin, Martin, *A Description of the Western Islands of Scotland*, p. 108-109, Published 1695.

[102] Martin, Martin, *A Description of the Western Islands of Scotland*, p. 110-111, Published 1695.

"Greagach and Glaistig"

"Gruagach, i.e. long-haired one, from gruag, a wig, is a common Gaelic name for a maiden, a young woman…The name evidently refers to the length of the hair, which it seems to have been a custom in ancient times for men of rank and freemen to allow to grow long. In Argyllshire, and commonly in Gaelic, the name gruagach (applied to the tutelary being haunting farms and castles) means the same as glaistig, and the idea attached to it is that of a long haired female, well-dressed like a gentlewoman, looking after the servants and particularly after the cattle. In parts of Skye, however, the fold-frequenting gruagach is a tall young man with long yellow hair in the attire of a gentleman of a bygone period, having a little switch (stalag) in his hand, and with a white breast as if he wore a frilled shirt…The gruagach was attentive to the herds and kept them from the rocks. He frequented certain places in the field where the cattle were. A gruagach was to be found in every gentleman's fold (buaile), and, like the glaistig, milk had to be set apart for him every evening in a hollow in some particular stone called clach na gruagaich ('the gruagach stone') kept in the bryes. Unless this was done no milk was got at next milking, or the cream would not rise to the surface of the milk. The Gruagach amused himself by loosing the cattle in the byre at night, and making people get out of bed several times to tie them up…on entering the byre, the gruagach was heard laughing and tittering in corners. Beyond this diversion, he seems to have been ordinarily harmless. He sometimes walked alongside people, but was never known to speak…" [103]

"Glaistig of MacQueen's Big Rock"

"Dr. Johnson mentions a 'Greograca' in Troda, an islet off the east coast of Skye. This Gruagach seems long since to have disappeared, but old people say the place is a very likely one for a being of the class to be in. At Holm (East Side) and Scorrybreck (near Portree) the stones where the libations were poured out may still be seen. In Braes the gruagach that

---

[103] Ronald Black, *The Gaelic Otherworld, John Gregorson Campbell's Superstitions of the Highlands and Islands of Scotland and Witchcraft and Second Sight in the Highlands and Islands*, p. 98-99, Birlinn Origin 2019.

followed the herds was a young woman with long hair; she was also known as the glaistig, and the rock in which her portion of milk was poured is in MacQueen's Big Rock – Creagan na Glaistig an Creag Mhor Mhic Cuinn." [104]

"'The Glaistig's Little Rock in MacQueen's Big Rock'. The location of this is uncertain. Peadar O' Donnghaile, Camustianavaig, tells me (personal communication, 10 November 2003) that when the Braes were surveyed in 1877 for the six-inch map published in 1882, the name 'McQueen's Rock' was wrongly given to Creag na Sgaillin, a long scree slope above the eastern spur of Beinn Tianabhaig." [105]

"Greogach in Troda"

"In Troda, within the[s]e three-and-thirty years, milk was put every Saturday for Greogach, or the Old Man with the Long Beard. Whether Greogach was courted as kind, or dreaded as terrible, whether they meant, by giving him the milk, to obtain good, or avert evil, I was not informed. The Mini[s]ter is now living by whom the practice was abolished." [106]

"Kenneth MacQueen's Buried Treasure"

"Kenneth MacQueen, who held the Cnogaire as tack in the 17th Century, was a man of considerable wealth. On his death-bed he told his family that he had concealed his wealth at the base of Cnogaire Hill. It could be discovered, when the Pleiades (grioglachan) were right above Marradh hill at a time when the moon was a certain angle above the same hill. At the time of MacQueen's death, his two white horses, with forelegs

[104] Ronald Black, *The Gaelic Otherworld, John Gregorson Campbell's Superstitions of the Highlands and Islands of Scotland and Witchcraft and Second Sight in the Highlands and Islands*, p. 100, Birlinn Origin 2019.
[105] Ronald Black, *The Gaelic Otherworld, John Gregorson Campbell's Superstitions of the Highlands and Islands of Scotland and Witchcraft and Second Sight in the Highlands and Islands*, p. 327, Birlinn Origin 2019.
[106] Samuel Johnson, *a Journey to the Western Islands of Scotland*, p. 247, Published 1791

tied together, were within thirteen steps of the spot. The treasure has never yet been discovered." [107]

Cruachan MhicSuain

A grass covered hilltop on Ben Tianavaig on the Isle of Skye. Cruachan MhicSuain is named after a Viking King. At the eastern base of Ben Tianavaig there is a small lake named McQueen's Loch.

Skye Dance called "America"

"We had again a good dinner, and in the evening a great dance…And then we performed…a dance which I suppose the emigration from Skye has occasioned. They call it "America"… It goes on till all are set a-going, setting and wheeling round eachother…It shows how emigration catches till all are set afloat. Mrs. Mackinnon told me that last year when the ship sailed from Portree for America, the people on shore were almost distracted when they saw their relations go off; they lay on the ground and tumbled, and tore the grass with their teeth. This year there was not a tear shed. The people on shore seemed to think that they would soon follow. [108]

---

[107] Ronald Black, *The Gaelic Otherworld, John Gregorson Campbell's Superstitions of the Highlands and Islands of Scotland and Witchcraft and Second Sight in the Highlands and Islands*, p. 408, Birlinn Origin 2019.

[108] James Boswell, Journal of a Tour to the Hebrides, ed. By Frederick A. Pottle and Charles H Bennett (New York, 1936), p. 242-243

The Murder of Thomas McQuain

The story varies between authors. The commonality and truth, however, is that Thomas McQuain, son of Duncan McQuain, was killed and his fortune made from selling apple brandy was stolen from him. Thomas McQuain was Hugh McQuain's cousin.

The killers were Confederate soldier imposters by the names of Lake and Harney. Thomas had befriended these two men for a number of days and during this time they had heard of his saved wealth. Thomas' intention with his saved wealth was to purchase some land as an investment in Augusta County, Virginia. In 1862, Thomas was shot in the back and arm while traveling alone on horseback with $1,500 in Confederate currency while in route to buy the investment farm. His money and horse were stolen and he died under a Spanish oak tree.

Lake and Harney were detained but both were able to escape custody.

In his memory, there has been a "Thomas" (first or middle name) in our family tree since his death.

<u>McQuain Brothers Bridge</u>

The McQuain Brothers Bridge is in Roane County, West Virginia and was commemorated for 11 McQuain Brothers that served in the Military during World War II and the Korean War. They are great-great grandchildren of Alexander II, with the exception of Donald Noe (who was the McQuain brothers' half-brother).

The 11 McQuain brothers, according to Senate Concurrent Resolution No. 39, are listed below:

First Sgt. John McQuain (Army)
Sgt. Ralph McQuain (Air Force)
Seaman 1-C Clyde McQuain (Coast Guard)
S-Sgt. Jack McQuain (Army) (Bronze Star/Purple Heart)
Cpl. Roy McQuain (Army) (German POW)
Coxswain Herbert McQuain (Navy)
Seaman 1-C Paul McQuain (Navy)
Seaman 1-C Gene McQuain (Navy)
PFC. Porter McQuain (Army)
George McQuain (Navy) (Purple Heart)
T-Sgt. Donald Noe (Air Force)

<u>Irish and Scottish Songs</u>

- *Wild Rover*- A popular Irish drinking song. It is an English language folk song of Scottish origin that is still commonly sung in Irish pubs today. The song dates back to late 16th century and is sung by fans of the Celtic Football Club in Scotland at away matches.
    - o My wife and I first heard this song in Cork, Ireland in 2019. The energy of the pub was unforgettable. Everyone knew the words and began to sing and clap.
- *Loch Lomond*- A beautiful Scottish traditional song sung in English which was published in 1841.
    - o It is possible that Alexander crossed Loch Lomond as a part of the recorded 30 families mentioned in this book that sailed across it while travel to the port at Greenock to sail for the New World.
- *The Skye Boat Song*- Scottish song (with English lyrics) written in the late-19th century. The song is about the journey of Bonnie Prince Charlie as he traveled from Benbecula to the Isle of Skye as he evaded capture by government troops after being defeated at the Battle of Culloden in 1746.
- *Tullochgorum*- a fast and uplifting melody with no lyrics that is cited as being played on the bagpipes by a gentlemen during the journey mentioned in this book by the 30 families traveling to the New World from Scotland.
    - o Thus, it is possible that Alexander McQuain listened to this very song while traveling with a large group in anticipation of his new life in America.
- *Mo Ghille Mear (My Gallant Hero)* - An Irish song sung in Irish. It is a haunting but beautiful lament to Scotland, the exile of the Bonnie Prince Charlie and defeat at Culloden.
    - o Since "McQuain" is a name of Irish origins and Scottish Highland origins, this song should strike an emotional chord in remembrance of brave lives lost while fighting for a concept that many Americans can sympathies with- freedom.
- *Cumha Mhic Shuain á Roaig* - An official tune of Clan MacQueen. It is a lament for MacSwain of Roag.

PICTURES AND
SCANNED RECORDS

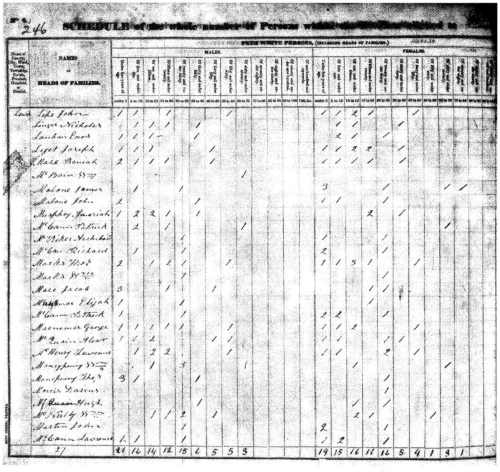

109

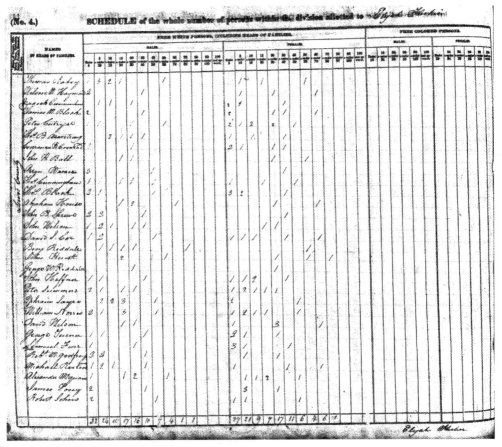

[110] 1840 Census (Alexander II is seen as head of household over 10 others).

SCHEDULE 1.—Inhabitants in _Troy Township_, in the County of _Gilmer_,
of _West Virginia_, enumerated by me on the _20th_ day of _July_, 1870.

Post Office: _Troy_   233

		The name of every person whose place of abode on the first day of June, 1870, was in this family.	Age	Sex	Color	Profession, Occupation, or Trade of each person, male or female.	Value of Real Estate	Value of Personal Estate	Place of Birth, naming State or Territory of U.S.; or the Country, if of foreign birth.							Whether deaf and dumb, blind, insane, or idiotic		
1	45 44	Montgomery William A	42	M	W	Farmer		500	Virginia									1
2		— Martha E	19	F	W	Keeping House			Virginia									2
3		— Wilmore P.	15	M	W	At home			Virginia							1		3
4		— Elizabeth R.	13	F	W				Virginia									4
5	46 45	Hunt James H	52	M	W	Farmer	500	30	Virginia									5
6		— Bebe M	51	F	W	Keeping house			Virginia									6
7		— John A.	27	M	W	Farm Laborer			Virginia							1		7
8		— Peter P	25	M	W				Virginia					1	1	1		8
9		— Jacob L.	19	M	W				Virginia							1		9
10		— James N	9	M	W				Virginia							1		10
11		Wagner Melvina E	16	F	W	At home			Virginia							1		11
12	47 46	McSwain Hugh	52	M	W	Farmer	2500	1000	Virginia								1	12
13		— Eunice	46	F	W	Keeping house			Virginia									13
14		— George M	19	M	W	Farm Laborer			Virginia							1		14
15		— Thomas C.	17	M	W	At home			Virginia							1		15
16		— Oliver C.	16	M	W				Virginia									16
17		— Nancy C.	14	F	W				Virginia									17
18		— Alexander M.	12	M	W				Virginia									18
19		— Columbia	10	F	W				Virginia									19
20		— Adam L	9	M	W				Virginia									20
21		— John E. H	7	M	W				West Virginia									21
22		— Mary H	4	F	W				West Virginia									22
23	48 47	Sandy George N	31	M	W	Farmer		100	Virginia							1	1	23
24		— Elizabeth	30	F	W	Keeping house			Virginia									24
25		— Lafayette N.	8	M	W				Virginia									25
26		— Harriet E.	6	F	W				West Virginia									26
27	49 48	Hesher Peter	63	M	W	Farmer	900	500	Virginia							1		27
28		— Malvina	46	F	W	Keeping house			Virginia									28
29		— James H	11	M	W				Virginia									29
30		— Harriet	9	F	W				Virginia									30
31		— Margaret R.	6	F	W				West Virginia									31
32		— Jeffrey	2	M	W				West Virginia									32
33	50 49	Ashenpack	58	M	W	Farmer	2000	1700	Virginia							1		33
34		— Elizabeth	50	F	W	Keeping house			Virginia									34
35		— Victoria	8	F	W				Virginia									35
36		Springston Sarah	18	F	W	At home			Virginia									36
37		— Liddie	16	F	W				Virginia									37
38	51 53	Montgomery Samuel	26	M	W	Farmer		150	Virginia							1	1	38
39		— Louisa	19	F	W	Keeping house			Virginia							1		39
40		McSwain Catharine	70	F	W				Virginia									40

No. of dwellings, 7   No. of white females, 19   No. of males, foreign born, ___
No. of families, ___   " " colored males, ___   " " females, ___
" " white males, 24   " " females, ___   " " blind, ___   No. of Insane, ___

111

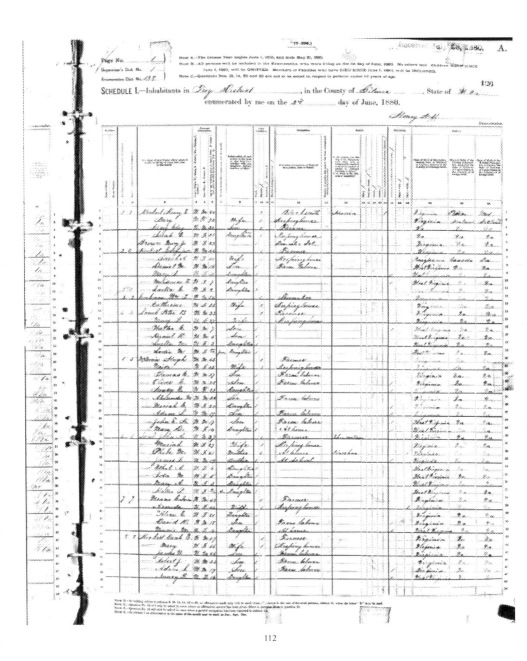

[112] 1880 Census (Hugh and Family are recorded).

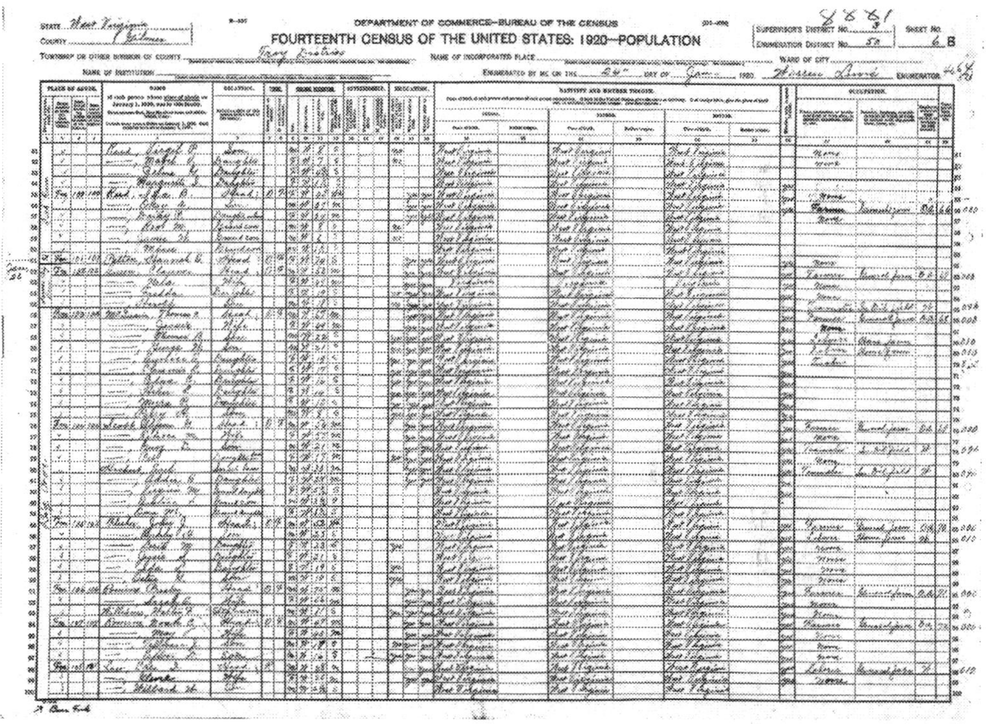
STATE West Virginia
COUNTY Gilmer
DEPARTMENT OF COMMERCE—BUREAU OF THE CENSUS
FOURTEENTH CENSUS OF THE UNITED STATES: 1920—POPULATION
TOWNSHIP OR OTHER DIVISION OF COUNTY Troy District
NAME OF INCORPORATED PLACE
NAME OF INSTITUTION
ENUMERATED BY ME ON THE 24th DAY OF Jan 1920
ENUMERATOR
SUPERVISOR'S DISTRICT NO. 3
ENUMERATION DISTRICT NO. 58
SHEET NO. 6 B
WARD OF CITY

113

113 1920 Census (Thomas Charles and family are recorded).

[114] 1940 Census (Thomas Bryan and family are recorded).

115

116

---

[116] Photo came from the barn of Bayward Butler. Scanned and emailed to me by Georgette Ward on July 1st, 2018. This photo is of Adam McQuain, son of Zan McQuain, on the right side. He was wounded in the 5th Marine Regiment in WWI. Thomas Bryan was at Parris Island at the same time as Adam, whose barracks was one over from his own.

Dr. John McQuain

Dr. J. E. McQuain's
Private Hospital

117

---

[117] Photo came from the barn of Bayward Butler. Scanned and emailed to me by Georgette Ward on July 1st, 2018. The picture is of Dr. John McQuain. He is mentioned in *West Virginia, In History, Life, Literature, and Industry*. His grandfather is Alexander II. His Father is Hugh McQuain. He was one of Thomas Charles' brothers.

118

ALEXANDER McQUAIN
C.1756 – C.1825
VIRGINIA MILITIA

REVOLUTIONARY WAR PATRIOT
SERVING IN
CAPT. PETER HULL'S CO.
BURIED 1.64 MILES
TO THE NW
38°30'7.74"N 79°25'31.21"W
IN AN UNMARKED GRAVE
ALONGSIDE HIS WIFE
MARY BODKIN McQUAIN
C.1766 – C.1803

Left to right; top row, Samuel McQuain, Iola McQuain, Robert McQuain, Margaret (Maggie) with daughter Lena, John McQuain, Kate McQuain, Middle row; William McQuain, John Marshall McQuain, Ida (Masters) McQuain, Bottom row; Ida (Melle) McQuain, Charles McQuain, Jane McQuain, Elizabeth (Betty) McQuain, and Nancy McQuain)

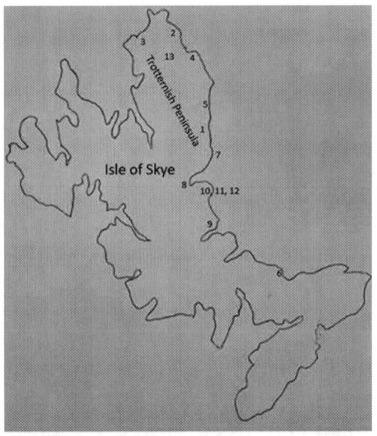

1. Storr, 2. Balmacqueen, 3. Kilmuir, 4. Garafad,
5. Rigg (close to An Eaglais Bhreige and A' Chubaid),
6. Broadford (close to Rudha an Eireannaich), 7. Holm Island,
8. Portree, 9. Braes (Close to Creagan na Glaistig an Creag Mhor Mhic Cuinn),
10. Cruachan MhicSuain, 11. Mcqueen's Loch, 12. Ben Tianavaig,
13. The Quirang

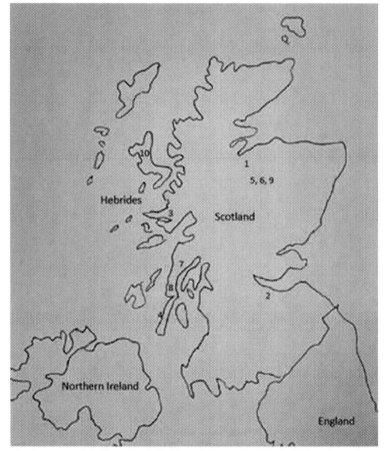

1. Inverness, 2. Edinburgh, 3. Moidart, 4. Kintyre Peninsula, 5. Corrybrough, 6. Findhorn, 7. Argyllshire, 8. Castle Sween, 9. Strathdearn, 10. Isle of Skye

Printed in the United States
By Bookmasters